Fleeing the Garden

PROCEEDINGS of the
MORMON THEOLOGY SEMINAR

THE PROCEEDINGS OF THE MORMON THEOLOGY SEMINAR series is based on a novel idea: that Mormons do theology. Doing theology is different from weighing history or deciding doctrine. Theology speculates. It experiments with questions and advances hypotheses. It tests new angles and pulls loose threads.

The Mormon Theology Seminar organizes interdisciplinary, collaborative, theological readings of Latter-day Saint scripture. Seminar participants with diverse backgrounds closely explore familiar texts in creative ways. In partnership with the Laura F. Willes Center for Book of Mormon Studies at the Neal A. Maxwell Institute for Religious Scholarship, the Mormon Theology Seminar presents these experiments upon the word to foster greater theological engagement with basic Mormon texts.

Series Editor
Brian M. Hauglid

Other MORMON THEOLOGY SEMINAR *books include:*

Adam S. Miller, ed.,
An Experiment on the Word: Reading Alma 32

Joseph M. Spencer and Jenny Webb, eds.,
Reading Nephi Reading Isaiah: 2 Nephi 26–27

Julie M. Smith, ed.,
Apocalypse: Reading Revelation 21–22

Jeremiah John and Joseph M. Spencer, eds.,
Embracing the Law: Reading Doctrine and Covenants 42

Fleeing the Garden

Reading Genesis 2–3

Edited by
Adam S. Miller

NEAL A. MAXWELL
INSTITUTE *for*
RELIGIOUS SCHOLARSHIP

Brigham Young University
Provo, Utah

A Proceedings of the Mormon Theology Seminar book

Neal A. Maxwell Institute, Provo 84602 | maxwellinstitute.byu.edu

Library of Congress Cataloging-in-Publication Data
Names: Mormon Theology Seminar (2013 : Utah Valley University), author. | Miller, Adam S., editor.
Title: Fleeing the garden : reading Genesis 2–3 / Adam S. Miller, editor.
Description: Provo, UT : Neal A. Maxwell Institute, 2017. | Series: Proceedings of the Mormon theology seminar series | Includes bibliographical references.
Identifiers: LCCN 2017036025 (print) | LCCN 2017043113 (ebook) | ISBN 9780842530101 (E-book) | ISBN 9780842530118 (Kindle) | ISBN 9780842530095 (print : alk. paper)
Subjects: LCSH: Eden—Congresses. | Bible. Genesis, II–III—Criticism, interpretation, etc.—Congresses. | Church of Jesus Christ of Latter-day Saints—Doctrines—Congresses. | Mormon Church—Doctrines—Congresses.
Classification: LCC BS1237 (ebook) | LCC BS1237 .M68 2013 (print) | DDC 222/.1106—dc23
LC record available at https://lccn.loc.gov/2017036025

∞ This paper meets the requirements of ANSI/NISO z39.48-1992 (Permanence of Paper).

ISBN 978-0-8425-3009-5

Cover and book design: Jenny Webb and Andrew Heiss

Printed in the United States of America

Contents

Introduction: On Biblical Literalism   vii

Paradoxes in Paradise   1
Julie M. Smith

"Adam, Where Art Thou?" Onomastics, Etymology,   31
and Translation in Genesis 2–3
Ben Spackman

Chaos and Order, Order and Chaos: The Creation Story   48
as the Story of Human Community
James E. Faulconer

Creation, Localism, and Appetite in the Garden World   68
of Wendell Berry
Rosalynde Welch

Theoscatology: On Dirt, Dung, and Digestion in God's Garden   82
Adam S. Miller

"And It Came to Pass": A Response to Adam Miller's   96
"Theoscatology"
Joseph M. Spencer

Partaking of the Fruit of Ecological Wisdom: A Reading   102
of Genesis 2–3 Applied to Environmental Education in Zion
Candice D. Wendt

Contributors   119

Introduction: On Biblical Literalism

THE TROUBLE WITH MANY "LITERAL" READINGS of scripture is that they ignore the letter of the text. These readings are literal only in a figurative sense. Biblical fundamentalism, for instance, rather than being conservative and literal, often depends on highly selective, thoroughly modern, and strikingly liberal readings of key texts. Why, then, is biblical fundamentalism associated with scriptural literalism?

In debates about scriptural interpretation, the word *literal* often just functions as shorthand for the claim that *the text refers to something real.* In such cases, the word is used without regard to *how* something is referenced—the designation of *how* a text refers being the kind of work the word *literal* is meant to do—and instead is used to stake a position on the *success* of a referential connection. In these debates, *literally* just means "really." Or, even more crudely, the word *literal* becomes shorthand for "true" and, conversely, the word *figurative* becomes shorthand for "false." To be literally true is to be really true. Then, saying that something is "only" figurative sounds like an attempt to dodge the question of reference or to soften or sugarcoat the verdict that what's being talked about is make-believe.

One basic problem with this way of talking is that it confuses two distinct issues. *How* a text refers—be it literally or figuratively—is no measure for the *success* of its referential connection. First, with respect to how reference works, it is important to recognize that *all* referential connections work by way of detour. Rather than connecting directly with a referent (with the object or idea in question), we connect with it indirectly by way of a web of words. We detour through language. Reference always involves this layer of indirection and third-party mediation. Terms like *literal* and *figurative* are meant to roughly measure the *size* of the detour that a given referential connection takes. The more common and familiar a referential detour is, the more literal we say the language is. The more circuitous and unconventional a referential detour is, the more figurative the language becomes. The difference between literal language and figurative language is one of degree, not kind. Both are complex, both are oblique, and both involve layers of mediation and redirection. Literal references that work by way of ordinary and familiar detours require minimal interpretive work. Figurative references that work by way of more complex detours may loop through several semantic layers and then require a recursive interpretive gesture. But whether the interpretive gesture is relatively simple or recursively complex, the capacity for real referential connection is the same.

The advantage of more literal language is that it can often hit its referential target with a minimal amount of fuss. But this simplicity is also its weakness. Figurative complexity can also be an advantage—otherwise we wouldn't bother with it—and this advantage isn't just window dressing. Figurative language can often pack *more* referential punch than literal language because its route *is* unfamiliar and because the wider arc of its complex detour loops more things into the referential grid from which it draws power. Because its detour is bigger, figurative language involves more elements. And because it involves more elements, it can gather a bigger crowd of witnesses. When successful, figurative language can often draw more power and precipitate a more substantial semantic cloud. Literal references, while simpler, tend to be thinner and less substantial.

Problems arise, though, when the ordinary and familiar detour of a literal reference depends on a referential terrain that we no longer share with the source material. This happens when, for example, the words we're reading come from a world that diverges from ours because it belongs to a foreign way of life, to a place that is far away, or to a time that is long past. A literal mode of reference gets both complicated and attenuated when what was ordinary and familiar to its original audience is no longer ordinary and familiar to us. A reference that functioned with relative simplicity and minimal detour in its own time and place may start to look more and more complex and figurative to our eyes.

This is the thing to watch for. And this is where the two senses of the word *literal* diverge. On one hand, we have *literalism* (as it's co-opted by biblical fundamentalism) as shorthand for the claim that *there are no worlds but the ordinary one present and familiar to us and all serious modes of reference refer only and directly to our familiar world*. On the other hand, we have *literality* as a name for just one among many modes of real reference that all operate by way of detour, a mode whose relative simplicity depends on its successfully connecting with one specific member of the set of possible worlds.

Fundamentalism co-opts literalism by denying the possibility of multiple worlds, of historical heterogeneity, and, in the end, of history itself. Fundamentalism ignores the letter of the text by ignoring the divergence of worlds. It treats past worlds as if they had not passed. It treats everything in the present tense: the only world in which real reference takes place is our present world. In this sense, fundamentalism is ahistorical. It tries to cheat the demands of time—and the delays and detours required for real referential connection—by imposing an illusion of temporal homogeneity. Fundamentalism denies that texts themselves have a history, and so, ironically, it ends up denying, in practice, the real historicity of the past worlds referred to in those texts.

Consider a literal reading of Genesis 1. What does the letter of the text claim? What kind of world does it show?

In the beginning, there is a watery chaos. God divides these waters in two by inserting a "firmament," a kind of solid dome that creates a bubble of air—the sky—between the water above and the water beneath. But sometimes the water above the dome still leaks through. This is rain. (In general, this biblical world looks something like a snow globe and heaven sits atop its sturdy dome.)[1] Then God gathers the water that remains on the floor of the dome into one place

---

1. I touch on this same topic from a less philosophical perspective in *Letters to a Young Mormon* (Provo, UT: Neal A. Maxwell Institute for Religious Scholarship, 2013), 51–56.

so that dry land can appear. Lights, like the sun and the moon and the stars, are installed in the roof of the dome and, set in intricate patterns, spin across its face. As God calls them into being, vegetation covers the dry land, fish swarm the sea, birds fill the air, and creeping things roam the plains.

Now compare this narrowly literal reading of the letter of the text with what popularly gets described as a "literal" reading. Take, for example, the highly imaginative and ahistorical way a contemporary film (like Terrence Malick's beautiful 2011 film, *The Tree of Life*) might visually represent the Genesis text. The setting will be dramatically different. Here, in the beginning, would be outer space, and space is filled with stars and nebulae and planets. The earth is a piecemeal ball of molten matter suspended in a vacuum. Its crust is dark and cooling, and it orbits a star against a backdrop of uncountable galaxies. The scene is volcanic. The planet's transformation is incremental, and it fills a nearly immeasurable amount of time as, gradually, life creeps into view and fills the earth.

Here, in this second case, the letter of an ancient Hebrew cosmology gets paired with high-end, twenty-first-century, CGI-powered render-ings of a contemporary pop cosmology. Were it to zoom across the film's frame, the starship *Enterprise* and its crew would look perfectly at home. Now, noting the odd pairing involved in this juxtaposition is not the same thing as objecting to it. But we shouldn't kid ourselves that it is a literal rendering of what the text communicates. It is, rather, a highly figurative transposition of an ancient cosmology that, by way of this transposition, makes a bid for contemporary relevance.

Contemporary relevance is not to be eschewed. But when read-ing old and exotic texts like the opening chapters of Genesis, it is the nature of that relevance that is at issue. Referentially, the text has two distinguishable targets: (1) its account of God's grace actively at work in the ordering of the world and (2) its account of the world that God's grace ordered. The very modern and highly imaginative fundamentalist reading takes the second target—that ancient Hebrew account of the world—as the thing that must be made present and relevant. But, because our world has diverged from that of the ancient Hebrews, fundamentalism can force a "literal" reading of the text only by systematically ignoring the letter of the text and supplying, instead, a reading that is extremely figurative. The worry is that if *their* ancient texts don't straightforwardly refer to *our* present world, then the reality of God's intervention in both worlds will be suspect. The irony is that, in their zeal to save the possibility of referential success for the second target (and then, by implication, the first), they risk compromising the text's ability to successfully connect with the first target: God. It is neither our place nor within our power to save that ancient Hebrew world from passing away. And, moreover, we need not save it in order to save the claim that God was willing to show himself in it. God can show his grace at work in whatever kind of world and in whatever span of time he likes. It's the showing of his grace that is decisive, not the continuity of worlds. And, more, it is the discontinuity of past worlds that weighs in favor of their actual historicity.

If, though, we are willing to let the text refer to a world that has passed away (to a Hebrew understanding of the world that is no longer given to us), then the text can become relevant to our redemption. No longer expending energy on downplaying the text's real history by pretending that the ancient Hebrews' world is straightforwardly assimilable to ours, we're free to focus our efforts on connecting with the referential reality of the first target: God's grace. The critical point of real referential continuity between the manifestation of God's grace in their world and the manifestation of God's grace in ours is *not the continuity of our worlds but the continuity of God's grace*. We don't have to fret about whether we share the same world. Rather, we have to worry about whether we share the same God.

This is the pivotal question: can an account of the real manifestation of God's grace in their lost world help make the reality of that ongoing grace more visible in ours? The degree to which this grace is manifest is the degree to which the text has revelatory force. Grace is the measure of a redemptive revelation.

Further, it is crucial to note that, often, figurative language can display the reality of God's grace with more referential force than literal language can and, importantly, that figurative language may move more easily between worlds. We may no longer think, as the Hebrews did, that the world is flat or that the sky is a solid dome, but there are aspects of how they *lived* in that world—the fabric of love, loss, anger, affect, light, sensation, and vulnerability—that remain common ground. And these aspects of life are often both the hardest to talk about and the most receptive to grace. Trying to connect with these translucent aspects of life, and trying to convey with real referential and revelatory force the nature of that connection, can require us to bend language into unusual shapes and employ it figuratively. But this resort to more figurative language is not a failure of reference. It is not a flight from truth into consoling poetic fantasies. Rather, it is a triumph of language's capacity to handle real truths by way of complex detours through thick semantic webs that can, as a result, fittingly represent something of the complexity and thickness of God's own grace as it quietly weaves its way through the fabric of worlds and lives.

The papers presented in this volume demonstrate a keen awareness of this complexity and are finely tuned both to the divergence of our world from the world of Genesis 2–3 and to the manifestations of God's grace that are nonetheless common to each of them. The specific set of papers included here is the product of a larger project called The Mormon Theology Seminar. The seminar is an independent scholarly forum dedicated to organizing short-term, collaborative readings of Mormon scripture that (1) offer close readings of key texts and (2) experiment with the potential theological implications of these readings.

This particular seminar took Genesis 2–3 as its text. The six seminar participants—three women and three men with diverse academic backgrounds—worked on a weekly basis through the details of Genesis 2–3, verse by verse and word by word, for three months. At the conclusion of the seminar's intensely collaborative work, the participants each chose an angle specific to their interests and training and drafted a conference paper based on that approach. A public conference presenting these papers was held at Utah Valley University in June 2013. The essays that follow are polished and expanded versions of these conference presentations.

The essays clearly show both a common core of understanding won through close collaborative effort and a wide diversity of methodological approaches and areas of interest. They range from a grammatical and philological examination of key technical terms in the Hebrew

text, to a philosophic
to practical reflection
mental stewardship. O
contemporary work in

comedy,
viron-
y of

Paradoxes in Paradise

Julie M. Smith

IN THE LAST FEW DECADES, two very different interpretive communities, each presumably unacquainted with the other's work, cast aside
the millennia-old interpretation[1] of Genesis 3 that found fault with
Eve's actions. They adopted the same innovative reading: Eve's choice
to eat from the fruit of the tree of knowledge of good and evil was
wise—an idea that I will call the Wise Choice Theory. No one would be
surprised that one of these groups consists of feminist biblical scholars;[2]
what may be a bit of a shock is that the other group is composed of
members and leaders of the LDS Church.[3]

---

1. For a general history of the interpretation of this passage, particularly in regard
to women's roles, see Jolene Edmunds Rockwood, "The Redemption of Eve," in *Sisters in
Spirit: Mormon Women in Historical and Cultural Perspective*, ed. Maureen Ursenbach
Beecher and Lavina Fielding Anderson (Urbana: University of Illinois Press, 1987).

2. See the pioneering work of Phyllis Trible, "A Love Story Gone Awry," in *God and
the Rhetoric of Sexuality* (Philadelphia: Fortress, 1978).

3. An excellent history of LDS interpretations of the fall can be found in Rico
Martinez's "Adam Fell That Men Might Be: An Exegetical History," a paper presented
at the eighth annual meeting of the Society for Mormon Philosophy and Theology,
September 22, 2012. Perhaps the classic statement of the Wise Choice Theory comes
from Elder Dallin H. Oaks: "It was Eve who first transgressed the limits of Eden in
order to initiate the conditions of mortality. Her act, whatever its nature, was formally
a transgression but eternally a glorious necessity to open the doorway toward eternal
life. Adam showed his wisdom by doing the same. And thus Eve and 'Adam fell that men
might be' (2 Nephi 2:25). Some Christians condemn Eve for her act, concluding that

1

Obstacles to the Wise Choice Theory

While the appeal of the Wise Choice Theory is obvious in an age of anxiety over women's[4] nature and roles,[5] there are many problems associated with this reading. I will explore these difficulties and then consider some other ways in which we might approach this most enigmatic of texts. I find nine major obstacles to the Wise Choice Theory.

---

she and her daughters are somehow flawed by it. Not the Latter-day Saints! Informed by revelation, we celebrate Eve's act and honor her wisdom and courage in the great episode called the Fall. Joseph Smith taught that it was not a 'sin,' because God had decreed it. Brigham Young declared, 'We should never blame Mother Eve, not the least.' Elder Joseph Fielding Smith said: 'I never speak of the part Eve took in this fall as a sin, nor do I accuse Adam of a sin.... This was a transgression of the law, but not a sin ... for it was something that Adam and Eve had to do!'" Dallin H. Oaks, "The Great Plan of Happiness," *Ensign*, November 1993, 72. For an LDS feminist application of the Wise Choice Theory to exonerate Eve (and, by extension, all women), see Alison Walker, "Theological Foundations of Patriarchy," *Dialogue: A Journal of Mormon Thought* 23/3 (1990): 77–89.

    4. In LDS thought the emphasis normally is on Eve as the one who made the wise choice, presumably because she was the one who assessed the fruit (Genesis 3:6) and ate first. However, in some articulations of the theory, Adam is given equal credit for his wisdom. (If we assume that Adam was offered the fruit first but refused it, we might ask if he was initially not as wise as Eve.)

    5. The Wise Choice Theory may perform the laudable work of removing the foundation for much of the misogyny that has historically been heaped upon women, oftentimes specifically rooted in this very story. (The classic example of this is found in the Wisdom of Sirach [a second-century-BCE collection of teachings that may be alluded to several times in the New Testament]: "From a woman sin had its beginning and because of her we all die" [Sirach 25:24].) At the same time, the theory promotes a brand of feminism that many find inadequate, inasmuch as it can be read to put Eve on a pedestal and to reinforce the legitimacy of men's leadership and women's maternal roles. (It is curious that Eve becomes a major model in LDS thought for women when Adam is rarely characterized as such for men.) Note that while most LDS interpretation since the mid-twentieth century has found a more expansive and positive role for Eve, there has been some retrogression as well: in the hymn "Sons of Michael, He Approaches," a line addressing Eve, "endless with thy Lord preside," was changed in the 1985 hymnbook to "endless with thy seed abide." See Douglas Campbell, "Changes in LDS Hymns: Implications and Opportunities," *Dialogue* 28/3 (Fall 1995): 65–91.

Reactions

Note the reactions to eating[6] the fruit: Adam and Eve hide from God (Genesis 3:8), they are afraid (v. 10),[7] they are ashamed,[8] and, most importantly, instead of proudly announcing their act when questioned,[9] they try to deflect blame (vv. 12–13). Further, when asked why she had eaten, Eve states that she had been tricked (v. 13).[10] These are

---

6. It is difficult to determine which parts of the story should be understood literally, which parts symbolically, or which parts as both. Brigham Young famously described the creation of Adam from the dust as "baby stories" (in *Journal of Discourses*, 2:6 [23 October 1853]), and Spencer W. Kimball taught that "the story of the rib, of course, is figurative" ("The Blessings and Responsibilities of Womanhood," *Ensign*, March 1976, 73; the *of course* in that statement is particularly interesting). One presumes that the actual sin was not eating per se (although some scholars have toyed with the notion of the fruit as poisonous or as a mind-altering substance; see Adam Miller's paper in this volume), but that the eating was, rather, symbolic. At the same time, LDS leaders have been adamant that Adam and Eve were literal, historical people. See "The Origin of Man," *Improvement Era*, November 1909, 75–81. This leaves us in the odd position of having historical people in symbolic stories; it is as if Jesus had stepped into one of his parables.

7. Only Adam is mentioned here, but I assume that Eve is also afraid since she has also hidden.

8. Compare Genesis 3:7 with Genesis 2:25. The possible symbolism of nakedness includes sexual awareness, awareness of sexual differentiation, lust, vulnerability, and shame. (There may also be a play on words, given that the word used to describe the serpent [*subtil* in Genesis 3:1] is virtually identical to the word translated as "naked.") But while the meaning of Adam and Eve's nakedness may be difficult to pin down, it does seem to be the result of having their eyes opened and obtaining the knowledge of good and evil. Is this what it means to be wise—to be aware of one's nakedness? Note also that, before the fall, God provides them with food and they do not require clothing; after the fall, God provides them with clothing but requires them to procure their own food. There is an intriguing inversion here. The inability to definitely pin down the symbolism of nakedness is another level of interpretive potential in this story.

9. Note that Adam and Eve are asked about their actions, but in the Genesis account the serpent is not. The reason for this lacuna is not made clear, but some interpreters have tied it to the fact that the story is not ultimately concerned with the origins of evil; presumably, asking the serpent what he had been doing would have given the reader more information about this origin. If this reading is correct, it implies that the author of the account is not particularly concerned with the ultimate origin of evil.

10. The KJV uses *beguiled*, a word normally translated as "deceived" when it occurs elsewhere (see, for example, 2 Kings 18:29 or Isaiah 19:13). Also note that *deceive* or

not the responses of people who think they have just done something wise. Additionally, the consequences[11] laid out for Adam, Eve, and the serpent read as if they are anything but a reward for having made a good decision;[12] consider the words directed at Adam: "Because thou hast hearkened unto the voice of thy wife, and hast eaten of the tree,

---

beguile in relation to Eve's action is used in multiple other scriptures across the canon (see 2 Corinthians 11:3; 1 Timothy 2:14; 2 Nephi 9:9; Mosiah 16:3; Ether 8:25; and Moses 4:19); nowhere is her decision described in clearly positive terms. It is difficult to determine precisely what the deception was, given that all the serpent did was ask a question (with, admittedly, an incorrect premise) and then make what appears to be a truthful statement regarding the consequences of eating the fruit. Perhaps the problem is that the serpent mentions only the positive consequences, not the negative ones, and also casts aspersions on God's motives. (David Bokovoy's reinterpretation of Satan's work to destroy agency as removing the *consequences* of human action instead of the *choices* presented to humans may be helpful here. See his paper "Agency in LDS Theology: A Misunderstood Concept?" at http://www.withoutend.org/agency-lds-theology-misunderstood-concept/.) It is also difficult to understand why God would prohibit Adam and Eve from gaining the knowledge of good and evil and becoming like the gods; we would assume that both of those things would be what God wanted for Adam and Eve. It is difficult to understand how someone who was deceived could have been making a wise choice. Even if the choice itself was a good one, the person would not deserve any credit for it.

11. These are traditionally called "curses," but note that only the serpent is cursed (Genesis 3:14); the ground is cursed for Adam's sake, but Adam himself is not cursed (v. 17), and the word *cursed* is not used in association with Eve (v. 16). Further, a reason is given for the consequences bestowed on Adam ("because thou hast hearkened unto the voice of thy wife, and hast eaten of the tree," but note that the account in Genesis does not involve Eve actually saying anything to Adam) and the serpent ("because thou hast done this"), but there is no explanatory clause when Eve's consequences are presented. Does that imply that what she has done wrong should be self-evident, or does it imply that she has done nothing wrong (but the serpent and Adam have)?

12. Although the curse that the serpent is given—particularly the enmity between the serpent and the seed of the woman (Genesis 3:15)—may be presented formally as a curse, it is in fact something of a blessing for Eve. (Why is the enmity between the serpent and the seed of specifically the woman and not the seed of both Adam and Eve? One interpretation is to read it as a reference to the only child who would be the seed of a woman but not a mortal man: Christ. If this is the best reading, it raises interesting questions about the text because it requires us to view Eve as a symbol for Mary and thus advances a much less literal interpretation of the text.) But note that it is still difficult to find justice in the serpent's being cursed for doing something that was necessary and appropriate and that led to a wise decision on Eve's part.

of which I commanded thee, saying, Thou shalt not eat of it: cursed is the ground for thy sake; in sorrow shalt thou eat of it all the days of thy life."[13] Note the reiteration of the command not to eat, the fact that eating has resulted in increased toil, and that listening to his wife is cast in a negative light. It is very hard to read God's reply to Adam as the response to a wise decision.[14]

---

13. There is an obvious sense in which the consequences for eating are very different for Adam and Eve, but it is also—paradoxically—true that the consequences have a deep similarity. Hugh Nibley explains, "Now a curse [*sic*] was placed on Eve, and it looked as if she would have to pay a high price for taking the initiative in the search for knowledge. To our surprise the *identical* curse [*sic*] was placed on Adam also. For Eve, God 'will greatly multiply thy sorrow and thy conception. In sorrow shalt thou bring forth children.' (Genesis 3:16.) The key is the word for sorrow, *atsav*, meaning to labor, to toil, to sweat, to do something very hard. . . . Both the conception and the labor of Eve will be multiple; she will have many children. Then the Lord says to Adam, 'In *sorrow* shalt thou eat of it all the days of thy life' (that is, the bread that his labor must bring forth from the earth). The identical word is used in both cases; the root meaning is to work hard at cutting or digging; both the man and the woman must sorrow and both must labor. . . . If Eve must labor to bring forth, so too must Adam labor (Genesis 3:17; Moses 4:23) to quicken the earth so it shall bring forth. Both of them bring forth life with sweat and tears, and Adam is not the favored party. If his labor is not as severe as hers, it is more protracted. For Eve's life will be spared long after her childbearing—'nevertheless thy life shall be spared'—while Adam's toil must go on to the end of his days: 'In sorrow shalt thou eat of it *all* the days of the life!' Even retirement is no escape from that sorrow." See Hugh Nibley, "Patriarchy and Matriarchy," in *Old Testament and Related Studies*, ed. John W. Welch, Gary P. Gillum, and Don E. Norton (Salt Lake City: Deseret Book, 1986), 89–90. There are additional similarities between the two: in Genesis 4, Eve will engage in naming and birthing activities similar to what Adam has done in Genesis 2–3. Similarly, immediately after Eve is created, what Adam focuses on is how very similar ("flesh of my flesh and bone of my bone," Genesis 2:23) she is to him. It is difficult to know where to draw the line on the similarities between Adam and Eve; for example, if Adam is created out of the ground and is to serve the ground (Genesis 2:5–7), does this imply that because Eve is created from the man that she is to serve the man? If so, does she serve him by convincing him to eat of the fruit (note that her creation immediately follows the command not to eat of the tree), or does she serve him after the fall, and, if so, how?

14. The same argument could be made for the consequences articulated for Eve and the serpent.

Disobedience

Note that Eve ate in direct disobedience to a clear commandment:[15] Genesis 2:16–17 reads, "And the Lord God commanded the man, saying, Of every tree of the garden thou mayest freely eat: But of the tree of the knowledge of good and evil, thou shalt not eat of it: for in the day that thou eatest thereof thou shalt surely die." It is nearly impossible to understand how direct disobedience to a commandment could have been a wise choice.

---

15. The situation is complicated by the fact that, in the Genesis account, Eve has not yet been created when this commandment is given (see Genesis 2:16–18). There are several ways to interpret this: (1) Adam or God later relays the commandment to Eve; (2) Eve and Adam form a unified human prior to her separation (although if this is true, how is it possible that Adam is "alone" [Genesis 2:18]?), so she is given the commandment in Genesis 2:17; or (3) Eve is not guilty of violating the commandment because it was never given to her. (Note that the second person singular form of the verb is used when the commandment is given.) This reading is further complicated by the idea that it appears to be possible for Adam to fulfill his life's work, tilling in the garden, while Eve, apparently, will need to leave the garden in order to have children. (There is perhaps room for interesting interpretive work in this misalignment of needs between Adam and Eve.) Before evaluating these options, we should note that (1) when Eve restates the commandment in Genesis 3:2–3, she makes several substantive changes to it and (2) the Hebrew of the Genesis account implies strongly that Adam was with Eve when she was speaking to the serpent and then eating the fruit. See Nahum Sarna, *JPS Torah Commentary: Genesis* (New York: Jewish Publication Society, 1989), 25. (The story feels very different if one envisions Adam standing there, a silent partner, neither objecting nor leading, while Eve talks to the serpent, evaluates the fruit, eats, and then offers Adam the fruit.) Further, the meaning of *die* (Genesis 2:17) is very difficult here, since Adam and Eve do not literally die in the day that they eat (which is doubly awkward since the serpent informed them correctly that they would not die when they ate; see Genesis 3:4) and would apparently not have died if God hadn't taken the additional step of cutting off their access to the tree of life (see Genesis 3:22–24; Alma 12:23 and 42:5–7 also seem to support this reading). Additionally, when Eve speaks to the serpent, neither she nor the serpent ever refers to the "tree of knowledge of good and evil," but simply to the tree "in the midst of the garden" (Genesis 3:3). The inability to determine (1) Eve's relationship to the commandment, (2) Adam's presence (or absence) at the scene, and (3) the meaning of *die* are three more paradoxes hiding behind the main paradox, which makes the story even more challenging to interpret.

Some interpreters have suggested that Adam and Eve faced conflicting commandments and had to choose "the higher law,"[16] but this
position has several drawbacks. First, it seems incompatible with the
nature of God to think that conflicting commandments could ever
be given.[17] Next, the other commandment—to multiply and replenish
the earth—comes in Genesis 1, which most scholars believe was written by a different author,[18] implying that neither account originally
had conflicting commandments;[19] that conflict came only later when
an editor stitched the two stories together.[20] Additionally, there is no
divine guidance given to Adam and Eve in the text that would lead
them to conclude that it was better to eat than to violate the other
commandment;[21] rather, it is not God but a serpent who encourages

---

16. This idea appears to have originated with John A. Widtsoe. See Martinez,
"Adam Fell That Men Might Be" (n. 3 above). It has also been advocated by Delbert L.
Stapley: "As we advance toward perfection, there will be higher laws revealed to our
understanding and benefit that will replace those of a lower order. This truth was first
taught to Adam and Eve in the garden of Eden, when the Lord gave them two choices:
(1) not to partake of the forbidden fruit (Genesis 2:16–17) and (2) to multiply and
replenish the earth (Genesis 1:28), which choices call for obedience to a lesser law or a
higher one. They chose to fulfill the higher law." See Delbert L. Stapley, "The Pangs of
Unlearning," Conference Report, April 1967, 30–34.

17. See Orson Pratt, "Celestial Marriage," *The Seer* 1/3 (Washington, DC, 1853),
45–47.

18. Most scholars believe that Genesis 1 was written by the "priestly" source and
Genesis 2–3 by the "Jahwist" source. See Robert Alter, "Composite Artistry," in *The Art
of Biblical Narrative* (New York: Basic Books, 1981).

19. Interestingly, there is no reference at all to the commandment to multiply and
replenish the earth in the Book of Mormon. Credit for this insight belongs to Rico
Martinez.

20. Some scholars point out that the conflict between the texts must not have been
perceived as overwhelming, else the redactor would not have been willing to place
the texts side by side. See James E. Faulconer, "Adam and Eve—Community: Reading
Genesis 2–3," *Journal of Philosophy and Scripture* 1/1 (Fall 2003): 2–16. See also Yamin
Levy, "Fiat and Forming: Genesis 1 & 2 Revisited," *Tradition* 27/1 (September 1992):
20–33. The redactor either did not notice the apparent contradiction or else was not
bothered by it.

21. In other texts where conflicting commandments *are* present, there is clear
divine guidance as to which commandment should be prioritized; see Genesis 22:2
and 1 Nephi 4:11.

them to eat. So there is no particular reason to think they made the better choice.

Further, there is a conflict only if one assumes that Adam and Eve could not have had children in the garden,[22] but that is a questionable assumption.[23] If God gave them the commandment to multiply (Genesis 1:28), we should presume they were able to fulfill it.[24] And it would have been odd if Adam and Eve had been created by God as part of a "very good" creation but had been, in effect, infertile; note that the text never claims they could not have children in the garden, and Eve's assessment of the fruit does not indicate that she expects to be able to have children only after she eats. Further, the statement that God would "multiply"[25] Eve's childbearing implies a baseline that is not zero. And the fact that Adam is expected to till the garden[26] implies that Eve can also complete her primary function—bearing children—in the garden

---

22. The argument was made by Orson Pratt. See Pratt, "Celestial Marriage," 45. The argument that Adam and Eve could have had children in the garden was presented in an LDS Church magazine in 1974. See Daniel H. Ludlow, "Q&A: Questions and Answers," *New Era*, September 1973, 13–14. And there is evidence when comparing revisions of LDS Church manuals to suggest that the church may be moving away from the view that Adam and Eve were able to have children only after they had left the garden. (The sentence "they were able to have children," which was included in the 1997 *Gospel Principles* manual as one of the results of the fall, was not included in the 2009 edition.)

23. One obstacle to this view is texts such as 2 Nephi 2:22–25 that seem to suggest that Adam and Eve could not have had children. One way to read these texts is that they apply only to the brief period when Eve had eaten but Adam had not, because her separation from Adam would have made it impossible for them to have children. Also note that 2 Nephi 2:23 says that they *would* not have had children, not that they *could* not. Interestingly, in this reading it is Adam who makes a "wise choice," and one profoundly different from the one that Eve makes. Hers is based on deception and focused on self-fulfillment, while his is made rationally and focused on the needs of their progeny. This reading highlights the fact that the Wise Choice Theory, when applied to Eve, seems to imply that Adam was foolish not to eat (although note that the Genesis text does not show Adam refusing the fruit at any point).

24. See 1 Nephi 3:7: "The Lord giveth no commandments unto the children of men, save he shall prepare a way for them that they may accomplish the thing which he commandeth them."

25. Genesis 3:16.

26. See Genesis 2:5.

as well. Additionally, some ancient interpreters have understood Genesis 1:28 not as a commandment to multiply and replenish the earth but rather as a blessing to be able to do so.[27]

What would have happened if they had stayed in the garden *and* had children? Would one of their descendants have eaten and been cast out?[28] Or might all of their descendants have stayed in the garden and experienced a mortality very different from ours?[29] What would have happened if Eve had eaten but Adam had refused? Would the plan have really been foiled, or would another woman have been created from another rib? Our inability to answer these counterfactuals presents yet another layer of complication in the effort to interpret the story.

Independent of Adam and Eve's fertility before the fall,[30] there are other problems with the theory of conflicting commandments, because it assumes that Adam and Eve were supposed to resolve the conflict on their own and not wait for further light and knowledge from God. Finally, and perhaps most seriously, if they had conflicting commandments, then there was no path that permitted obedience: either they ate so they could have children (violating the commandment not to eat), or they didn't eat and didn't have children (violating the commandment to multiply).[31] This raises profound concerns about the nature of

---

27. It should be noted that there is a long and strong tradition in LDS interpretation to view God's words in Genesis 1:28 as a commandment.

28. Perhaps the inverse of the principle articulated in Esther 4:14 ("For if thou altogether holdest thy peace at this time, then shall there enlargement and deliverance arise to the Jews from another place") is relevant here: had Adam and Eve not eaten, someone else—one of their children—would have.

29. Many purposes of mortal life—such as being tested and tried (after all, the fruit and the serpent were there), forming families, and having a body—could all have been accomplished in the garden, assuming that Adam and Eve could have had children there. (The one thing they would not have needed was a Redeemer, however.)

30. Note that the Hebrew Bible does not call this story "the fall"; the case could be made that this title overinterprets the text, but I use it because it compensates in pithiness for what it lacks in accuracy.

31. The tensions here are well articulated as a question in *Answers to Gospel Questions*: "Was the 'Fall' inevitable and necessary to the human race? Our whole hope of salvation rests on the character of God the Father, does it not? If he is just and consistent we are secure. If he is unfair or changeable we have no security. If God ever gave man

God to think that humans would be placed in a position where disobedience was the only option. It is frequently argued that conflicting commandments were required in order for Adam and Eve to exercise their agency, but it does not seem that this would be the case: with just one commandment, they still had the choice of keeping it or of violating it, and so agency is preserved.[32]

Another explanation that the Wise Choice Theory offers to the problem of the prohibition has to do with finding a distinction between a sin and a transgression,[33] but there are a few problems here as well: there is nothing in God's commandment that would lead to the conclusion that a violation would be only a transgression.[34] Also, the distinction between the two does not appear to exist in all scriptures.[35] But even if we were to assume a distinction, it is still not clear

---

contradictory commandments did he not at that point rob man of his free agency? We are repeatedly told we are free to choose between good and evil; between obedience and disobedience; but if a situation was set up in which two commandments contradict each other, then man [Adam] was free to choose only between two disobediences. Is that fair? If God 'framed' man and then cursed him and punished him for something he could not help doing, what assurance have we that when we do our very best we won't find ourselves cursed and cast out for doing the very thing God meant us to do? Is this justice? Is that free agency?" Joseph Fielding Smith, *Answers to Gospel Questions* (Salt Lake City: Deseret Book, 1957), 2:211.

32. Would Adam and Eve have been tempted to eat had the serpent not been there? The story functions perfectly well without Genesis 3:1–5.

33. This idea was articulated by Orson F. Whitney in his *Saturday Night Thoughts*, part 3 (Salt Lake City: Deseret News Press, 1921), 92. It has also been taught recently by Dallin H. Oaks. See his article "The Great Plan of Happiness," *Ensign*, November 1993.

34. As Rico Martinez explains, "Further complicating [this interpretation] is the fact that the legal concept . . . historically appealed to Natural Law or divine law. What could be more 'divine' than God commanding Adam not to eat of the forbidden fruit? How can an express command by God be given the same status as a municipal ordinance? This is an odd ripple in a nascent Mormon jurisprudence." See Martinez, "Adam Fell That Men Might Be."

35. See, for example, Ezekiel 18:30, Isaiah 59:12, Psalm 32:1, 2 Nephi 9:46, Mosiah 2:40, Acts 1:25, D&C 109:34, and especially 1 John 3:4 for instances where there appears to be no distinction between a sin and a transgression. This analysis is, admittedly, complicated by the various languages behind these texts. And note that even those who advocate the distinction between a sin and a transgression, such as Dallin H. Oaks,

that a transgression could ever be deemed wise. So despite arguments that there were conflicting commandments or a distinction between a sin and a transgression,[36] there are problems with the Wise Choice Theory stemming from the fact that Adam and Eve were commanded not to eat.

History of interpretation

The Book of Mormon does not appear to support, and many nineteenth-century LDS interpreters did not subscribe to, the Wise Choice Theory.[37] The Book of Mormon mentions the role of the serpent in causing mankind to become "lost"[38] and emphasizes that the fruit was

---

acknowledge that not all scriptures make a distinction between the two terms. See Oaks, "Great Plan of Happiness."

36. There also appears to be a contradiction between both the "conflicting commandments" theory and the "it was a transgression, not a sin" theory and D&C 29:34–35, where the Lord explains, "Not at any time have I given unto you a law which was temporal; neither any man, nor the children of men; neither Adam, your father, whom I created. Behold, I gave unto him that he should be an agent unto himself; and I gave unto him commandment, but no temporal commandment gave I unto him, for my commandments are spiritual; they are not natural nor temporal, neither carnal nor sensual." While there are many ways of interpreting the words *temporal, spiritual, carnal,* and *sensual,* most interpretations would not permit the concept of a "transgression" or the idea of conflicting commandments, especially given the language used later in this passage that seems to prohibit the notion that the fall was a wise decision: "The devil tempted Adam, and he partook of the forbidden fruit and transgressed the commandment, wherein he became subject to the will of the devil, because he yielded unto temptation. Wherefore, I, the Lord God, caused that he should be cast out from the Garden of Eden, from my presence" (D&C 29:40–41).

37. In other words, this is an innovative theory. That does not make it automatically wrong, especially in a church that believes in continuing revelation, but it does mean that the Wise Choice Theory is not an inherent or integral part of the restoration. And while it is widely taught now and appears in most official church publications that mention the fall, it does not appear to meet some of the more commonly used criteria for what constitutes "official" Mormon doctrine, given that it has not been authoritatively taught by a prophet. On the other hand, it might be considered official if the criteria are (1) repeatedly taught by members of the Quorum of the Twelve and (2) present in multiple official church publications.

38. Mosiah 16:4.

"forbidden."[39] The most positive statement about the fall in the Book of Mormon is "Adam fell that men might be; and men are, that they might have joy."[40] But note that while the Book of Mormon usually speaks of Adam and Eve as a unit, here Adam is mentioned separately. It is possible that Adam's decision to eat is qualitatively different from Eve's. In fact, there is a long LDS interpretive history, now largely forgotten, rooted in 1 Timothy 2:14[41] (which states that Eve was deceived but Adam was not), arguing that Adam made a wise (or neutral) choice after Eve made a foolish choice.[42] Nineteenth-century Latter-day Saints

---

39. See 2 Nephi 2:15, 18–19; Mosiah 3:26; and Helaman 6:26. Alma 30:25 can also be interpreted to suggest that the Nephites taught the idea of original sin.

40. 2 Nephi 2:25.

41. Contra 1 Timothy 2:14, several Book of Mormon texts (2 Nephi 9:9; Mosiah 16:3; Ether 8:25) seem to imply that Adam was also "beguiled." The previous verses in 1 Timothy appear to argue that Eve is inferior because she was created second (some subscribers to the Wise Choice Theory have argued that 1 Timothy is inaccurate [see, for example, Beverly Campbell, *Eve and the Choice Made in Eden* (Salt Lake City: Bookcraft, 2003), 73]). Contrast this view with Gordon B. Hinckley's statement that he liked "to regard Eve as [God's] masterpiece after all that had gone before" (see Gordon B. Hinckley, "Daughters of God," *Ensign*, November 1991) for a sense of the variety of competing interpretations that this text has been marshaled to support. There's also an interesting echo here with LDS discourse contra the larger tradition of biblical studies: in the world of biblical studies, the first text is usually presumed to be more accurate, but given the belief in modern revelation, Latter-day Saints make no such assumption—it may well be the later text that better reflects the will of the Lord. Sequence is thus no guarantor of superiority in a text, or in order of creation.

42. For example, Orson Pratt said, "Did Adam partake of this forbidden fruit, being deceived as Eve was deceived? Or did he partake of it knowingly and understandingly? I will give you my views upon this subject. Adam very well knew that his wife Eve, after she had partaken of the forbidden fruit, having transgressed the law of God, must die. He knew this; he knew that she would have to be cast out of the garden of Eden, from the presence of her husband; she could no longer be permitted to dwell with him. Hence, inasmuch as there was a great separation threatened between husband and wife—the wife having transgressed—he concluded that he would not be separated from the woman, and hence he was not deceived, but the woman was deceived; he partook of the forbidden fruit to prevent a separation between the two, and fell, even as the woman fell, and both were cast out together. If one only had transgressed and been cast out, the great command that had been given prior to that time—to multiply and replenish the earth—could not have been fulfilled, because of the separation. In order, therefore,

often spoke of "Eve's curse,"[43] and so in the earliest layers of LDS interpretation, Eve's choice was not seen as wise.[44] While there are several
nineteenth-century voices advocating that we do not blame our first
parents,[45] it would be a stretch to conclude from any of these statements
that Eve had made a wise choice, although one can certainly see the
trajectory that led future interpreters to the Wise Choice Theory.[46]

---

that the command first given might be fulfilled, Adam, though not deceived, partook
of the forbidden fruit, was cast out with Eve, and hence began, as far as possible, to
fulfil the command, and to multiply his species upon this earth." See Orson Pratt, in
Journal of Discourses, 26:290–91 (18 July 1880). See also George Q. Cannon, in *Journal
of Discourses*, 26:182–93 (28 September 1884). See also Brigham Young, in *Journal of
Discourses*, 6:142–49 (27 December 1857). Adam's choice would be justified in part by
the language of Genesis 2:24–25, which affirms Adam's duty to "cleave" unto his wife,
and perhaps this explains why, when God asks him what he has done, Adam refers to
the fact that "the woman *whom thou gavest to be with me*" ate (Genesis 3:12, emphasis
added), forcing him to eat if he wanted to stay with her. If this reading is correct, Adam
is the one more concerned with progeny than Eve, which is an interesting challenge
to current gender norms and the aspects of the Wise Choice Theory that make Eve
primarily focused on having children. Adam's decision would also have been substantially different from Eve's if he had watched Eve eat without dying; that puts the Lord's
promises and the serpent's claims in an entirely different light by providing empirical
evidence to support the serpent's claims but not the Lord's.

43. See Brigham Young, in *Journal of Discourses*, 12:93–98 (30 June 1867) and
15:129–35 (18 August 1872). In both of these instances, Brigham Young uses the concept of the curse of Eve (particularly the idea of the woman's desire being toward her
husband) to argue that women should accept polygamy. See also Susanna Morrill, *White
Roses on the Floor of Heaven: Mormon Women's Popular Theology, 1880–1920* (New York:
Routledge, 2006), 59. See also George Q. Cannon, in *Journal of Discourses*, 13:197–209
(9 October 1869).

44. Brigham Young said, "The Lord knew they would do this and he had designed
that they should." See Brigham Young, in *Journal of Discourses*, 10:307–14 (10–13 June
1864). Note that the Lord's foreknowledge of an event doesn't necessarily imply approval
of it. Also, there remains a conundrum: How could it have been part of the Lord's plan
for them to disobey God and follow Satan?

45. One such example is Brigham Young, who taught, "I will not blame Adam or
Eve." See Brigham Young, in *Journal of Discourses*, 10:312 (10 June 1864).

46. John Taylor said, "I have no complaints to make about our father Adam eating
the forbidden fruit, as some have, for I do not know but any of us would have done
the same." See John Taylor, in *Journal of Discourses*, 1:223 (8 April 1853). This is clearly

The Redeemer's role

The reading of the fall in the Book of Mormon implies another concern with the Wise Choice Theory: where the Book of Mormon writers were able to find anything positive in the fall, it stemmed not from Eve's eating the forbidden fruit but from the mercy God showed to Adam and Eve by sending them a redeemer. A major problem, then, with the Wise Choice Theory is that it draws perilously close to eliminating the need for a redeemer. While the foibles and failures of scriptural characters may make us uncomfortable, they also point to the need for a savior,[47] and minimizing their faults leads to a minimized need for redemption.

Focusing on the role of a redeemer might also help us better understand Eve's words in Moses 5:11, a text frequently used to defend the Wise Choice Theory: "Were it not for our transgression we never should have had seed, and never should have known good and evil, and the joy of our redemption, and the eternal life which God giveth unto all the obedient."[48] When read in context, what Eve is celebrating is not her decision to eat the forbidden fruit per se, but rather God's decision to provide a redeemer after she ate. To the extent that we make Eve the hero of this story, we risk erasing the redeemer's heroic role.

---

a move away from blaming Adam and Eve, but not quite the same as regarding the decision as wise.

47. For an example of how the idea that Adam and Eve had done something wrong is necessary to the need for a redeemer, consider this statement from Spencer W. Kimball: "Our first parents, Adam and Eve, disobeyed God. . . . In order for Adam to regain his original state (to be in the presence of God), an atonement for this disobedience was necessary. In God's divine plan, provision was made for a redeemer to break the bonds of death. . . . Jesus of Nazareth was the one who, before the world was created, was chosen to come to earth to perform this service, to conquer mortal death. This voluntary action would atone for the fall of Adam and Eve and permit the spirit of man to recover his body, thereby reuniting body and spirit" (Spencer W. Kimball, "The True Way of Life and Salvation," *Ensign*, May 1978). Had Adam and Eve not done anything "disobedient" or "forbidden," there would be no need for an atonement.

48. While this statement is usually accepted as accurate, one wonders if that is a safe assumption. Is Eve completely reliable here? Did she not have a veil drawn over her when she left the garden?

Accountability

It seems impossible that a decision made before consuming "the fruit of the tree of knowledge of good and evil"[49] could be regarded as good or evil;[50] it would, by definition, be morally neutral if Adam and Eve lacked the capacity for good and evil.[51]

The serpent's role

The eating is done not at the behest of God but at the prompting of the serpent. How can Satan[52] be the instigator of a wise choice? Moroni 7:17

---

49. There are various possibilities for what the fruit of the tree of knowledge of good and evil might symbolize: moral knowledge, "the experience of everything," omniscience, the consequences of obeying (that is, Eve knows good if she obeys and she knows evil if she does not), sexual knowledge (which is one of the few possible dimensions to the story that LDS readers have consistently dismissed). See Gordon Wenham, *Word Biblical Commentary: Genesis 1–15* (Waco, TX: Word, 1987), 63. See also Deuteronomy 1:39 and 2 Samuel 19:36. Regardless of the forbidden fruit's precise connotation, there are several thorny issues here: (1) It is difficult to understand why God would not want Adam and Eve to have the knowledge of good and evil. (2) As Reuven Kimelman explains, "Did she lack such knowledge? In actuality, before she ate, Eve was capable of telling the serpent about the interdiction, who prohibited it, and the dire results. Now, if one knows what is wrong, the authority behind it, and the consequences, where is the deficiency in the knowledge of good and evil?" See Reuven Kimelman, "The Seduction of Eve and Feminist Readings of the Garden of Eden," *Women in Judaism: A Multidisciplinary Journal* 1/2 (1998). (3) Contemplating eating the fruit becomes functionally the same as eating the fruit, inasmuch as it represents a choice with good and evil dimensions; as Leon Kass explains: "To reach for the forbidden fruit is already to have tasted it." See Leon Kass, *The Beginning of Wisdom: Reading Genesis* (New York: Free Press, 2003), 65. (4) Why isn't this tree called "the tree of death," which would nicely parallel "the tree of life" and which seems to be a good explanation for its effects? The inability to get an adequate grasp on what the fruit symbolizes is one of many paradoxes underlying the main paradox in the story.

50. Second Nephi 2:5 reads, "Men are instructed sufficiently that they know good from evil." But would this have been true before the fall?

51. See Bruce R. McConkie, *Mormon Doctrine* (Salt Lake City: Bookcraft, 1979), 735.

52. Note that the Genesis text does not make any association between the serpent and Satan; the serpent is just another animal created by God (although, according to

seems to address this: "After this manner doth the devil work, for he persuadeth no man to do good, no, not one." Viewing Eve's decision as wise requires us to erase the role of the serpent from the story, an ironic move given that the uniquely LDS accounts of the fall feature a much-expanded role for Satan relative to the Genesis text. If eating the fruit was simply part of the plan, why is the serpent even there? As with the danger of erasing the Redeemer, the Wise Choice Theory risks erasing Satan.

Alternatives

Some readers support the Wise Choice Theory because there was no other way for humanity to be introduced into the world.[53] There are two problems here. One is that performing a necessary but sinful task does not make one wise: one of the immediate causes of Jesus's death was Judas's betrayal, but this would not lead anyone to think that Judas had

---

Leviticus 11 and Deuteronomy 14, snakes are unclean). Later interpretations, including those in the Book of Mormon and the Book of Moses, do make the connection (see 2 Nephi 2:18; Moses 4:6). Some readers have suggested that Eve's inability to recognize that Satan—and not just another friendly animal—was actually speaking to her lies behind the deception. (Another variation of this theme is that Eve thought she was speaking to Jesus Christ, who is sometimes symbolized by a serpent, as in Helaman 8:14–15; in this reading, Christ tells Adam and Eve that because he will atone for them, they will not die. This is certainly contrary to the Book of Mormon's understanding of the story [e.g., Mosiah 16:3] and cannot explain why God would forbid them to eat, but it does present one coherent explanation for the role of the serpent under the Wise Choice Theory.) Yet this feels like an insufficient vindication of Eve, given that she clearly recognizes in her dialogue with the serpent that she has been commanded not to eat of the fruit (see Genesis 3:3). Further, it is difficult to understand why God would leave two innocent beings alone in the garden with the serpent. (For more on the paradoxical role of Satan in Mormonism in general and particularly in this story, see Jeffrey M. Bradshaw and Ronan James Head, "Mormonism's Satan and the Tree of Life," *Element* 4/2 [Fall 2008]: 1–52.) Another difficult issue: How is it possible that this serpent is permitted to be in the garden before the fall, but Adam and Eve are not allowed to stay in the garden after the fall? The ambiguity of the serpent's status combined with God's permission for the serpent to tempt the humans is yet another conundrum in the Genesis text.

53. See, for example, Campbell, *Eve and the Choice Made in Eden*, 27.

made a wise choice.[54] Second, thinking there was no other way to enter the world means adopting the serpent's assumptions, not God's—it is the serpent who implies there was no other way; God is silent on the matter. But since God is in the garden with Adam and Eve, they will presumably gain more knowledge in the future. Perhaps another choice would have presented itself had they just been patient.[55] There may be a helpful parallel[56] to the near sacrifice of Isaac in Genesis 22: in that story Abraham's willingness to keep the commandment that he was given led—but only at the last possible minute—to divine intervention that eliminated the need to violate a commandment. Had Adam and Eve refused to eat, would they have similarly had their eyes opened to a ram in the thicket that would have made progression without disobedience possible? One wonders if, once more time had passed and Adam and Eve had been taught more, they would have been offered the fruit by God. This is speculative, but it is also appealing because it makes better sense of God's prohibition; forbidding them to gain knowledge of good and evil and to be like the gods is difficult to understand if it were a permanent prohibition, but makes more sense as a temporary restriction. It is also possible that some other way of obtaining mortality that did not involve eating the fruit could have been introduced; perhaps the fruit is something of an illegitimate shortcut—a "magic pill"—that claims to offer the benefits of knowledge but in fact does not. (Note that the extent of their newfound knowledge seems to be nothing more than the shame-filled awareness that they are naked.) Another possibility is that they ate not too soon but from the wrong hand—not

---

54. As James E. Talmage wrote, "The sacrificial death of Christ was ordained from before the foundation of the world, yet Judas who betrayed . . . the son of God [is] none the less guilty of the awful crime" (James E. Talmage, *Articles of Faith* [Salt Lake City: Deseret Book, 1899], 63).

55. There may be a parallel to Sarah's insistence on solving her fertility problem by giving Hagar to Abraham (which the Genesis account seems to present as a mistake, although D&C 132:34 takes a different approach) instead of waiting for God to fulfill the promise.

56. See "Eve and Abraham," http://www.patheos.com/blogs/faithpromotingrumor /2011/11/eve-and-abraham/, although that author draws different conclusions from the parallel than I do here.

eating was a test of obedience that they failed; at any point, God could have offered them the fruit and it would have been acceptable to eat it. Our inability to know what would have happened had they chosen not to eat constitutes another interpretive conundrum.

Parallels to Genesis 4

There are important parallels between the fall and the very next chapter in Genesis, the sad story of Cain and Abel, with over a dozen thematic and verbal similarities.[57] For example, God says to Eve, "Thy desire shall be to thy husband, and he shall rule over thee,"[58] and to Cain, "Unto thee shall be his desire, and thou shalt rule over him."[59] Given these similarities, it is difficult to see Eve's decision as wise unless one is willing to view the murder of Abel in the same way.

The message

Finally, the Wise Choice Theory creates enormous problems for the normative use of the story.[60] One can appreciate the problem by imagining explaining to a Sunday School class of sixteen-year-olds that sometimes it is better to listen to what Satan wants you to do, even if it is in direct conflict with a specific commandment from God. We may choose to abandon the prescriptive value of the story, but it is difficult

---

57. See Thomas L. Brodie, *Genesis as Dialogue* (New York: Oxford University Press, 2001), 144. See also Kimelman, "Seduction of Eve," 2.

58. Genesis 3:16.

59. Genesis 4:7.

60. Which parts of the story should be treated as normative—and what norms they advance—is complicated. Note that the only explicitly normative statement is in Genesis 2:24: "Therefore shall a man leave his father and his mother, and shall cleave unto his wife: and they shall be one flesh." Is this verse included because it is the only part of the story meant to create a norm? (The fact that there is no evidence for matrilocality in ancient Israel makes this passage all the more intriguing.) Are the consequences of the fall (painful childbirth, hard labor, men's rule, etc.) meant to be normative, or are humans supposed to try to overcome them and live as they did in God's presence?

to imagine how we can maintain it if we argue that disobedience can be wise.[61]

Assessing the paradox

For these nine reasons, I find the Wise Choice Theory to be unsatisfactory. Yet viewing Eve's choice as morally neutral or as sinful is just as problematic. If we try to view the choice as neutral, we still need to grapple with the fact that it is in direct violation of a commandment. How can violating a commandment be morally neutral? And how can a neutral action lead to such a negative outcome?[62] On the other hand, if we view eating the fruit as sinful,[63] it seems incongruous that the

---

61. Similarly, if one argues that eating the fruit was a one-of-a-kind situation in its requirement for disobedience, then the normative use of the story has implicitly been abandoned.

62. Perhaps Adam and Eve's innocence meant that the entire blame should be placed on the serpent, but the serpent is there only because God permitted Adam and Eve to be alone with it, and so we are then in effect blaming God. That idea is obviously an uncomfortable one and is augmented by the fact that the serpent is more of a truth teller than God is (God does not tell them that their eyes will be opened if they eat; the serpent does, and God later verifies that this is indeed the case). Ultimately, there are only four characters—God, the serpent, Adam, and Eve—upon whom blame (if "blame" is indeed what we have here) can be bestowed. Yet neither individually nor in any combination can an adequate apportioning of blame be made. There are also interesting questions related to the fact that God puts Adam and Eve into a position where they are, in effect, left alone with a smooth talker and a really appealing but forbidden tree (which God created!), and yet they also lack the awareness to assess either the messenger or the consequences of their actions. How can that be part of a good creation? Why would God permit the serpent to dwell in paradise in the first place? (On the other hand, Leon Kass suggests that there was no way to have the garden without the tree—humans could not be created without agency. See Kass, *Beginning of Wisdom*, 68. In fact, it is immediately after the command not to eat is given that God announces the need for Adam to have a "help meet"; one wonders if the entire purpose of Eve's creation (at least in the narrative) is related to the issue of eating the fruit. (But is her job to help him eat the fruit or to prevent him from eating the fruit?) The issue of what our interpretations of the story reveal about the nature of God is another moving part that makes the meaning of the text difficult to pin down.

63. Feminist readers might object to seeing the first act of the first woman as sinful. But it is also true that the reading of Eve as brave and wise (and yet subjugated and

signal act of the first humans—people who will later be described as "glorious"[64] and "great and mighty"[65] and who, in Mormon teaching, are not mere mortals—was a sin. It would also be difficult to explain why human progression would *require* a sin. And in terms of Latter-day Saint thinking about the plurality of worlds,[66] we would find it inexplicable that each world would have required the same inaugurating sin.[67] Further, wouldn't God be in some sense responsible for the sin, since Adam and Eve were left alone with a wily serpent[68] and an unguarded

---

maternal) is problematic. Our ability to see Eve as committing a sin and then being redeemed makes her into a normal human, one with agency and autonomy. By way of analogy, a society that can only accept members of a formerly oppressed minority being portrayed in the media as virtuous doctors and lawyers, and not the full spectrum of human endeavor and occupation (including criminals, low-status workers, etc.), is a society that has not yet fully integrated that minority into society but rather feels the need to compensate for past (and current?) injustices by placing the minority in a privileged position.

64. D&C 138:39.

65. D&C 138:38.

66. See Hollis R. Johnson, "Worlds," in *Encyclopedia of Mormonism* (New York: Macmillan, 1992), 1595.

67. However, if the same script, as it were, had been playing out on multiple worlds, one wonders why Satan would agree to keep playing the same role that permits the plan to move forward, especially if we consider the idea in the Book of Moses that Satan acted only because "he knew not the mind of God" (Moses 4:6). (Possibly, Satan regarded Adam and Eve as pawns whom he would need to sacrifice in order to have a chance to influence their children. If this is true, it is a further problem for the Wise Choice Theory because it would mean that Eve made a "wise choice" for *her* that left her children in a terrible position.) In the context of a plurality of worlds, we have yet one more paradox in this story.

68. Some readers point to D&C 29:39–40 ("And it must needs be that the devil should tempt the children of men, or they could not be agents unto themselves; for if they never should have bitter they could not know the sweet—wherefore, it came to pass that the devil tempted Adam") as evidence that the serpent was merely playing the role that God had assigned to it. To the extent that this is true, it raises difficult and interesting questions about God's ultimate culpability (and Adam and Eve's lack thereof) for the decision to eat the fruit. Also, this verse does not seem to require that Adam and Eve eat, only that they be tempted. Presumably their agency would have been preserved in the presence of a temptation that they resisted.

tree?[69] And how could they sin *before* they had knowledge of what was good and what was evil?

There is a paradox at the center of this story since there is no satisfactory determination as to whether Eve's choice was wise, neutral, or sinful. No interpretation of her act can make sense of all the data. This state of affairs is particularly striking given that Latter-day Saints have not only the Genesis text but additional accounts of the fall unique to the restoration of the gospel: the Book of Moses,[70] the Book of Abraham,[71] and the temple ceremony.[72] Not one of these accounts eliminates the paradox.[73] One suspects that if the goal had been to remove the tension, at least one of the four accounts would have done it;[74] the fact that

---

69. Contrast the unguarded tree of knowledge of good and evil with the tree of life, in which cherubim and a flaming sword physically prevented Adam and Eve from eating its fruit (Genesis 3:24). One wonders why similar measures were not taken to prevent them from eating from the tree of knowledge of good and evil.

70. See Moses 4.

71. There is not a complete account of the fall in the Book of Abraham, but Abraham 5:13 does present an opportunity (that was not taken) to eliminate the paradox.

72. For a comparison of the various accounts, see Anthony A. Hutchinson, "A Mormon Midrash? LDS Creation Narratives Reconsidered," *Dialogue* 21/4 (Winter 1988): 11–74. Keith Meservy suggested some of the benefits of having multiple accounts of the creation; see his article "Four Accounts of the Creation," *Ensign*, January 1986.

73. Joseph Fielding Smith wrote, "Adam and Eve therefore did the very thing the Lord intended them to do. If we had the original record, we would see the purpose of the fall clearly stated and its necessity explained." Joseph Fielding Smith, *Answers to Gospel Questions* (Salt Lake City: Deseret Book, 1963), 4:80. One wonders why one of our four accounts—including the three that are products of the restoration—did not restore the parts of the record that clearly explained the fall.

74. Defenders of the Wise Choice Theory point to two changes that the Book of Moses makes to the Genesis text to support their position. The first is Moses 4:6, which states that Satan sought to beguile Eve, "for he knew not the mind of God." While this explains Satan's role in furthering God's plan (something that we would not normally expect him to do), it does not exonerate Eve. (And one still wonders what "the mind of God" was in this instance.) The second is the addition of "nevertheless, thou mayest choose for thyself, for it is given unto thee" (Moses 3:17) to the commandment not to eat the fruit. (See James E. Faust, "What It Means to Be a Daughter of God," *Ensign*, November 1999, as an example of using this verse to argue that eating the fruit was "a choice with consequences" and not "forbidden," an argument frequently made by defenders of the Wise Choice Theory.) This addition, however, is not sufficient to negate

the tension remains weighs in favor of reading it as intentional. Biblical scholar Robert Alter suggests that Genesis 3 is a carefully designed work, purposefully presenting the audience with multiple, incompatible viewpoints because that is the best way to tell a story about a world composed of incompatible facets, a world where truths are in tension.[75]

Perhaps the story invites us to accept the idea that we cannot understand everything that God can understand.[76] Maybe it is like Heisenberg's uncertainty principle: as soon as we decide that Eve made a wise choice, we are left wondering what role the serpent is playing. But if we begin with the role of the serpent, it is difficult to understand why God set the situation up this way. Because both aspects of the story cannot make sense at the same time, we enter into Eve's role, facing two trees but allowed to eat from only one of them. Our own efforts to make sense of the universe are inadequate; human reason ultimately fails. Given our limited understanding, we need to have faith that the story is something that God understands. We hope that someday an explanation will be made manifest. We have been given an opportunity to exercise charity as others unfold interpretations that seem inadequate to us since no single interpretation can embrace all of the data.

Note that the story never asks us to assess Eve's act; we are the ones who have decided that we must determine what is good and what is evil. But isn't the point of this story that making such a determination is God's job, and that it is only under the influence of Satan that Eve sets aside God's assessment of the fruit to make her own judgment?[77]

---

the basic prohibition of the commandment; it is easier to see this if we imagine the same verbiage applied to a different commandment: "Do not kill; nevertheless, thou mayest choose for thyself, for it is given unto thee." The phrasing serves only to emphasize the existence of agency and not to imply tacit permission to violate the commandment.

75. Robert Alter, *The Art of Biblical Narrative* (New York: Basic Books, 1981), 145–46.

76. See Mosiah 4:9.

77. Some feminist interpreters have pointed to Genesis 3:6, where Eve's threefold evaluation of the fruit is presented as evidence of her logical and careful thinking, but we should not forget that she is making this assessment contrary to the assessment of God. A wrinkle to the story is added by the Book of Moses, which has the fruit *becoming* pleasant as Eve ponders it (see Moses 4:12), as opposed to the Genesis text, where the fruit simply *was* pleasant (Genesis 3:6). This change might simply reflect Joseph Smith's

Are we doing the same thing when we attempt to judge her act?[78] And doesn't the story itself suggest that good and evil are bound together and cannot be separated?[79]

A text with a conundrum at its core points to the inadequacy of texts to solve problems, which prevents us from making idols out of texts and acknowledges the reality of what Joseph Smith called "the little, narrow prison, almost as it were, total darkness of paper, pen and ink;—and a crooked, broken, scattered and imperfect language."[80] It suggests an awareness of the complications of the world we live in. It also allows an interpretive flexibility that permits the text to be relevant to more than one situation.[81] No one text can encapsulate all truth. This one contains that truth precisely because of its inability to contain all truth.

This may sound a little too postmodern for an ancient text. But it is the very same message found in the book of Job, which has several compelling parallels to the story of the fall, not the least of which is a rare appearance of "the adversary"[82] and a story that demands to know whether the protagonist has done something wrong.[83] After Job has

---

penchant for eliminating italicized words in the KJV, but it might indicate that Eve's act of evaluating the fruit for herself (instead of relying on God's evaluation) made the fruit seem more pleasant than it was initially. Also, many advocates of the Wise Choice Theory think of Eve as selflessly willing to fall in order to have children, but her analysis of the benefits of eating the fruit does not support this notion.

78. The near-obsession with judging Eve's act may be due to the story's centrality, but it may also reflect a willingness to judge women in ways that men are normally not judged. For example, Luke 7:39 ("for she is a sinner") has generated many discussions about the nature and extent of the woman's sins, while a similar comment regarding a man in Luke 5:8 ("depart from me, for I am a sinful man") generates minimal discussion about the nature and extent of Peter's sins.

79. It is really most curious that this is the tree of good *and* evil, when so many scriptural texts work hard to present good and evil as opposing or divergent forces.

80. Joseph Smith, *History of the Church*, 1:299.

81. The history of LDS interpretations of the fall illustrates this, from Brigham Young's reading of Eve's curse as a justification for female submission to polygamy to the Wise Choice Theory as evidence that the LDS Church exalts women, at least when they fulfill certain roles.

82. See Job 1.

83. See Job 4.

begged God for an explanation of his suffering despite his innocence,[84] God's response is as simple as it is unexpected: it is not for Job to know. The solution belongs to God, and Job will not be given the information[85] that will explain the paradox of a righteous person suffering. Job must accept the uncertainty. This is the lesson of Eden's paradox as well.

Alternative templates

This is not to suggest that we abandon efforts to interpret the fall, only that we redirect our gaze from the question of good and evil and look in other directions, at the other trees in the garden. And there are many other templates through which we might consider Genesis 3:

1. It is a symbolic representation of the premortal experience of each human.[86] In this reading, eating the fruit is the choice to come to earth, made by each person. And perhaps our inability to weigh Eve's decision indicates that we simply don't have enough knowledge about the premortal life to understand how these decisions were made.[87]

2. The story presents the maturation of every human being, from a child who uses language to name animals, to awareness of sexual differentiation, to what we might today call teenage rebellion, to the effort to establish oneself as an

---

84. See Job 31.

85. See Job 37:1–40:2.

86. This interpretation is perhaps supported by this statement from Gordon B. Hinckley: "We have sketched before us [in the temple ceremony] the odyssey of man's eternal journey from premortal existence through this life to the life beyond." See Gordon B. Hinckley, "The Salt Lake Temple," *Ensign*, March 1993. This reading makes sense of the serpent being in the presence of God (as Satan in the premortal realm). It also may explain why, before the fall, the serpent (contrary to the usual artistic representation) did have legs—it is only after he is cursed that he moves about on his belly; this may be read symbolically to suggest that the serpent lost something (such as the ability to have a body) as a result of his role in the fall (symbolizing the war in heaven).

87. It is somewhat troubling to think that we would have had to disobey a commandment in order to come to earth, so the tension in the story is definitely still there in this template.

adult free from parental influence.[88] In this reading, eating the fruit is not primarily the one-time act of a historical woman but is, rather, emblematic of the effort all people individually make to differentiate themselves from their parents.

3. The garden is the first temple; there are several Hebrew words that strengthen this connection.[89] In this view, eating the fruit amounts to violating one's priestly stewardship;[90] this is why Adam and Eve are replaced as temple guardians by the cherubim and tasked with reestablishing the temple in a mortal realm. Here, eating the fruit is clearly a violation, but God mercifully provides an opportunity to be redeemed from it.

4. Adam and Eve represent Israel, permitted to live in the holy land so long as they follow God's commands but banished to Babylon when they are disobedient.[91] This reading makes sense of the story in the history of Israel.

---

88. See Hutchinson, "A Mormon Midrash?," for more on this idea of reading the temple ceremony in particular as the journey of "every(wo)man": "Clearly, the Adam and Eve of the endowment were intended as mythic personages in the strictest sense: in representing Everyman and Everywoman's search for religious truth and authority, they symbolically mediate the meaning and value—indeed, the truth—that Joseph's theology of revelation, priesthood order and authority, and exaltation to Godhood attempted to phrase propositionally." In the "human maturation" reading, the fact that Eve eats first probably signifies nothing more than the fact that females usually physically mature before males.

89. For example, regarding the commandment in Genesis 2:15, Bruce Waltke notes, "Elsewhere in the Pentateuch this expression describes activity only of priests." See Bruce Waltke, *Genesis: A Commentary* (Grand Rapids, MI: Zondervan, 2001), 87.

90. In this reading, we have a logical explanation for Eve's addition of a prohibition on touching the fruit to the original command: it fits in with the holiness codes, where one must not touch something unclean. See P. Wayne Townsend, "Eve's Answer to the Serpent: An Alternative Paradigm for Sin and Some Implications in Theology," *Calvin Theological Journal* 33/2 (1998): 399–420. See also Gregory K. Beale, "Eden, the Temple, and the Church's Mission in the New Creation," *Journal of the Evangelical Theological Society* 48/1 (March 2005): 5–31.

91. A benefit of this reading is that it explains where Cain's wives came from: there is no assumption that Adam and Eve were the first and only people but rather the first and

5. Eve is a symbol for the church, and Adam is a type of Christ. This reading emphasizes the distinction between their acts: Eve eats out of rebellion while Adam, as Christ, deliberately and righteously chooses the incarnation in order to stay with Eve.[92] This approach has the benefit of making Christ central to the temple endowment.[93]

6. The story reflects the conflict that exists within each person. In this reading, the desire for obedience and the desire for advancement wrestle within each soul.

Each of these templates presents its own panoply of possibilities.[94] All of them turn down the heat on the gender issues that typically boil over in discussions of the fall.[95]

In addition to thinking about various templates for the story, we find fertile ground in considering other scriptural texts that resonate with the fall. It is frequently noted by interpreters that Adam and Eve are not mentioned again in the Hebrew Bible after the first few chapters

---

only people in the promised land. Exile (out of the garden, out of the promised land) is "death"; being created from the dust means being people "of the land." The abundance and freedom of the garden symbolize "the land flowing with milk and honey." See Peter Enns and Jared Byas, *Genesis for Normal People: A Guide to the Most Controversial, Misunderstood, and Abused Book of the Bible* (Patheos, 2012), Kindle edition.

92. See Alonzo L. Gaskill, *The Savior and the Serpent: Unlocking the Doctrine of the Fall* (Salt Lake City: Deseret Book, 2005), 110–25.

93. It also changes the implications of Adam "ruling" over Eve and Eve "desiring" Adam; these are no longer commentaries on the husband/wife relationship but rather on the Christ/church relationship.

94. This perhaps isn't an entirely separate template, but note that, in the Genesis account, we are told that Adam is put to sleep but not that he awakes. This has led one scholar to interpret the entire fall account as a dream or vision. See Dan E. Burns, "Dream Form in Genesis 2:4b–3:24: Asleep in the Garden," *Journal for the Study of the Old Testament* 12/37 (February 1987): 3–14.

95. Perhaps given the current upheavals concerning gender roles, there is no way to escape inflicting our anxiety into discussions of the fall. But note that it is not required by the text that there be a commentary on male and female and/or husband and wife roles; after all, no one looks at Cain and Abel in the next chapter as a template for sibling relationships.

of Genesis,[96] but this does not imply that there are no allusions to the story or intriguing intertexts. The list of passages that might be intertexts for the fall is extensive:

1. Genesis 4 (Cain and Abel), which is discussed above.
2. Genesis 9 (Noah and his sons) involves nakedness and a curse.
3. Genesis 11 (the Tower of Babel) features the theme of transgressing boundaries to become "like God."
4. Numbers 22 (Baalam) is the only other canonical account of an animal with the power of speech; intriguingly, this story also features the opening of eyes and concern as to what constitutes evil and sin.[97]
5. 1 Samuel 3–5 (Eli's sons) features temple workers who should be symbolically in the presence of God but who eat forbidden fruit and die for it.
6. Ezekiel 28 (prophecies against kings and kingdoms) seems to refer to the garden story and has some interesting comments about sin.
7. 2 Samuel 11–14 (David and Bathsheba) can be read as David's fall with regard to Bathsheba.[98]
8. Proverbs 9 explores themes of wisdom, good, and evil, and it also features a woman who invites others to eat (Proverbs 9:5; where the KJV has *bread*, the underlying word could be translated as "food"). Might we see Eve in the wise woman of Proverbs?
9. The Song of Songs has been thought to be a commentary on Genesis 2–3.

---

96. Technically, Adam is mentioned in 1 Chronicles 1:1, but this is only a brief mention in a genealogical list.

97. See George W. Savran, "Beastly Speech: Intertextuality, Balaam's Ass and the Garden of Eden," *Journal for the Study of the Old Testament* 19/64 (December 1994): 33–55.

98. See P. G. Camp, "David's Fall: Reading 2 Samuel 11–14 in Light of Genesis 2–4," *Restoration Quarterly* 53/3 (2011): 149–58.

10. There are also several stories in the scriptures that place women in the role of providers of food (Sarah, Abigail, the widow of Zarephath, Mary and Martha), which might make for some interesting comparisons to the fall.

11. There appears to be a pattern in the Hebrew Bible where males are usually the main actors but females usually initiate actions; this pattern might include Eve, Sarah, Hannah, Tamar, Deborah, and others. The genealogy of Jesus in the book of Matthew might fit as well,[99] along with the overall scriptural pattern of women being present whenever there is a story narrated of someone being raised from the dead.

12. Matthew 4 (the temptations of Jesus) appears to have some resonances with Eve's threefold assessment of the fruit.[100]

13. Luke 15 (the parable of the prodigal son) might be compared with the fall; we might see Eve as the prodigal child who must reject parental authority, live in a fallen world, and then choose to come home.

14. Luke 24 (the road to Emmaus) features disciples who have "their eyes opened" when they consume food; there may be deliberate allusions to the story of (an inverted?) fall there.[101]

15. Revelation 21–22 (the new heaven and earth) features many resonances with and inversions of the fall.[102]

16. 1 Nephi 4 (Nephi beheads Laban) may be parallel to the Genesis account of Adam and Eve since both narratives feature "conflicting commandments" at the beginning of a volume, setting the tone for an entire text.

---

99. See Julie M. Smith, "Why *These* Women in Jesus' Genealogy?," *Segullah: Writings by Latter-day Saint Women* (Spring 2008).

100. See C. John Collins, *Genesis 1–4: A Linguistic, Literary, and Theological Commentary* (Phillipsburg, NJ: P & R Publishers, 2006), 186–88.

101. See Dane C. Ortlund, "'And Their Eyes Were Opened, and They Knew': An Inter-canonical Note on Luke 24:31," *Journal of the Evangelical Theological Society* 53/4 (2010): 717–28.

102. See Julie M. Smith, "The Beginning and the End: Echoes of Genesis 1–3 in Revelation 21–22," in *Apocalypse: Reading Revelation 21–22*, ed. Julie M. Smith (Provo, UT: Neal A. Maxwell Institute for Religious Scholarship, 2016), 15–30.

17. 1 Nephi 8 and 11 (Lehi's and Nephi's visions) feature trees, eating fruit, and issues of good and evil choices.
18. Alma 30 (Korihor) features a person through whom Satan is speaking in an attempt to deceive others.
19. Noncanonical ancient accounts might also shed more light on the story.[103]

It may also be fruitful to think about "the missing mother" in this account: the fact that Adam gives birth to Eve calls attention to the fact that there is no Mother God in the story. At the same time, it is also possible to read Genesis 2:24 as a reference to a divine female, the mother whom Adam leaves. If they hadn't eaten, would Adam and Eve have had some connection with their Mother in Heaven?[104] Could the serpent even be read as a symbol for the divine female, guiding her daughter? Some scholars have suggested that the tree of life is a symbol for female divinity;[105] given that Eve's name means "life," the connections here are thick and tempting. Considering other templates, other scripture texts, and the role of the divine feminine might help us better consume the story, without the distraction of assessing good and evil.

By way of conclusion, I share an incident from the life of David O. McKay, as related by Boyd K. Packer:

> When he was in his nineties, perhaps 94, he came to a temple meeting with all of the General Authorities. . . . On this occasion, President McKay . . . stood and put his big, bony hands across his chest, and he began to quote

---

103. For a comparison of Genesis with the story of Gilgamesh, see John A. Bailey, "Initiation and the Primal Woman in Gilgamesh and Genesis 2–3," *Journal of Biblical Literature* 89/2 (June 1970): 137–50. For a comparison with the Qur'an, see Torsten Löfstedt, "The Creation and Fall of Adam: A Comparison of the Qur'anic and Biblical Accounts," *Svensk Missionstidskrift* 93/4 (2005): 453–77. Perhaps the most important insight from the noncanonical intertexts is that no other ancient Near East creation account mentions the creation of women.

104. Is Isaiah 50:1 ("for your transgressions is your mother put away") relevant here?

105. See Daniel C. Peterson, "Nephi and His Asherah," *Journal of Book of Mormon Studies* 9/2 (2000): 16–25, 80–81.

> the endowment in the temple. . . . Then he stopped, and
> he looked at the ceiling for quite a few minutes, and he
> said, "I think I am finally beginning to understand."[106]

What I see in President McKay's statement that he was "finally beginning to understand" is the recognition that the interpretation of the
fall is neither easy nor obvious. In fact, there is no other story in the
canon that permits so many possible interpretations yet so resists all
interpretations. While the advancement of the Wise Choice Theory
has perhaps been a necessary corrective to a tradition that blamed and
shamed Eve, and therefore all women, it unfortunately cannot account
for several key features of the text. I argue that no one interpretation
of the fall can accommodate all of its facets, so we will be better off
reveling in the ambiguity of the text and considering other templates
through which to view the account.

---

106. Boyd K. Packer, "A Teacher of Teachers," *McKay Today Magazine*, Fall 2006, 5.

"Adam, Where Art Thou?" Onomastics, Etymology, and Translation in Genesis 2–3

Ben Spackman

Introduction

To OPEN THE SEMINAR AND PROMPT GENERAL DISCUSSION, I posted a loose translation of Genesis 2–3, which I termed an "impressionistic campfire retelling."[1] As with most modern translations, and in particular two literary translations by Robert Alter and Everett Fox, the proper name Adam[2] disappeared from my translation.[3] As noted by one of the other participants, the loss of Adam in translation "drastically changed the mood and feel of the text."[4] Should *'adam* be translated as a proper name in Genesis 2–3? If not, what does it mean there, and how should it

---

1. Available at http://genesisseminar.wordpress.com/2013/01/10/overview-of-genesis-2-3-part-1/.

2. Hereafter Adam will refer to the proper name and *'adam* to the general Hebrew term.

3. Robert Alter, *The Five Books of Moses: A Translation with Commentary* (New York: W. W. Norton, 2004); Everett Fox, *The Five Books of Moses: Genesis, Exodus, Leviticus, Numbers, Deuteronomy*, The Schocken Bible, vol. 1 (New York: Schocken Books, 1995).

4. Rosalynde Welch, email message to author, April 8, 2013.

be translated? Among the related challenges in translating these chapters is how best to represent the Hebrew ambiguities, wordplays, and relationships centering on the noun *ʾadam,* which plays multiple roles. In particular, I will discuss the translational issues with *ʾadam* and the ground, *ʾadam* in connection with the binaries of man/woman/male/female, and the tradition of Adam as a proper name. If Adam is not a proper name in this primary passage, how and when did it become so?

Proper names in Hebrew

In order to understand why Adam as a proper name has disappeared from most contemporary translations, a brief introduction to grammatical aspects of Hebrew proper names is necessary. First, proper names in Hebrew do not take the definite article (a prefixed *ha-*),[5] just as proper names in English do not take the definite article (e.g., "I went to work with Bob and Jennifer," not "I went to work with *the* Bob and *the* Jennifer").[6] Words with the definite article are therefore highly unlikely to be proper names.

Second, rules of capitalization vary from language to language. German capitalizes all nouns, and English only proper nouns. Capitalization assumes not just the priority of writing (one cannot hear capitals),[7] but a writing system that contains two tiers of letters, majuscules and minuscules. As with other Semitic scripts, Biblical Hebrew

---

5. Proper names are definite by definition. Paul Joüon and T. Muraoka, *A Grammar of Biblical Hebrew* (Rome: Editrice Pontificio Istituto Biblio, 1991), §137b. However, a regular noun with the article may be proper by extension, for example, *hayʾor,* "the River" = the Nile. Christo H. J. van der Merwe, Jackie A. Naudé, and Jan H. Kroeze, *A Biblical Hebrew Reference Grammar* (Sheffield, England: Sheffield Academic Press, 1999), §24.4.ii.e.

6. Exceptions tend to be foreign, such as The Hague. By contrast, proper names in Classical Greek, for example, regularly take the definite article.

7. In the oral presentation of this paper, I distinguished between Adam and *ʾadam* by giving the former the typical English pronunciation and the latter the typical Hebrew pronunciation.

has no capitalization at all, so proper nouns cannot be identified that way.[8]

Third, personal names in English today are pleasing connections of sounds and associations, often with archaic but largely irrelevant meanings that parents typically discover in baby books. By contrast, names in Hebrew have meaning because they were, for the most part, normal everyday words, such as Jonah, "dove," or phrases with God as the subject, such as Ishmael, "God has heard."[9] When calling King David by title and name, a person would be saying "king beloved one," the meaning of the sounds *melekh daweed*. This practice, combined with the lack of capitalization or any other formal marker of proper nouns, means that translators occasionally disagree over whether a given noun should be translated as a proper name or as its semantic equivalent in the target language. For example, the KJV twice assigns sons to a man named Hammelech. Because *hammelech* means "the king," most Bibles today translate that meaning, resulting in two sons of "the king" instead of two sons of a man named Hammelech.[10]

Lastly, since we will be considering the meaning of several Hebrew terms, a brief note on methodology is required. Meaning is determined by context and usage. For a linguist, philologer, or translator dealing with ancient languages, etymology is the last resort but also highly important. It is the last resort in determination of meaning for two reasons. First, words that appear to be closely related may not be; there is often a good bit of etymological uncertainty. Second, etymology is an unreliable indicator of meaning. Words shift meaning over time, and the meaning of a word often becomes completely unrelated to its origins. For example, knowing the meanings of both *butter* and *fly* does

---

8. Other languages have developed different ways of indicating proper names in writing. For example, Akkadian (i.e., Assyrian and Babylonian) writes the DINGIR sign before divine names, and two other optional signs indicate male and female personal names. See John Huehnergard, *A Grammar of Akkadian* (Winona Lake, IN: Eisenbrauns, 2000), §13.3.

9. An accessible selection of names and meanings is found in Jay A. Parry and Donald W. Parry, "Israelite Names—Witnesses of Deity," *Ensign*, December 1990, 52–54.

10. Jeremiah 36:26; 38:6. The prefixed *ha-* is the definite article, a strong indicator that the word is not a proper noun.

not contribute any understanding to the word *butterfly*. When we call someone "nice," we do not mean "ignorant," though that is the Latin origin of the term.[11]

Etymology is nevertheless quite important. Just as being a native speaker of English does not make me an English professor, the Hebrew writers were not Semiticists. They often attributed real-world significance to similar-sounding words based on apparent relation, referred to in the scholarly literature as folk etymologies. That is, the authors perceived such words, regardless of actual linguistic relationship, as related and used that perceived relationship as fodder for theological or other interpretations. Genesis 25:26 provides one example: "Afterward, his brother came out, with his hand gripping Esau's heel; so he was named Jacob."[12] Nahum Sarna comments on this passage.

> By folk etymology, the name is here derived from Hebrew
> *ʿakev*, "heel." In reality, Hebrew *yaʿakav* stems from a
> Semitic root *ʿ-k-v*, "to protect." It is abbreviated from a
> fuller form with a divine name or epithet as its subject.
> *Yaʿakov-ʾel*, "May El protect," is a name that has turned
> up several times in cuneiform texts over a wide area. The
> name Jacob is thus, in origin, a plea for divine protection
> of the newly born—most appropriate for the one who was
> to live his entire life in the shadow of danger.[13]

ʾadam as a proper name

While English speakers are most familiar with the proper name Adam, this is the rarest of its three usages in the Hebrew Bible. In appendix 1, I list all occurrences of *ʾadam* in the first column and grammatical

---

11. See the "Root Fallacy" section in D. A. Carson, *Exegetical Fallacies*, 2nd ed. (Grand Rapids, MI: Baker Academic, 1996), 28.

12. New Revised Standard Version (Nashville: Thomas Nelson, 1989). Hereafter abbreviated NRSV.

13. Nahum M. Sarna, *Genesis: The Traditional Hebrew Text with the New JPS Translation*, The JPS Torah Commentary (Philadelphia: Jewish Publication Society, 1989), 180.

determinedness in the second. Because Hebrew proper names do not take the definite article, only those occurrences that are indefinite or ambiguous have the possibility of being a proper name, which allows only four passages: Genesis 2:5, 2:20, 3:17, and 3:21. Outside these four passages, Adam is highly unlikely to be a proper name in Genesis 2–3 without violating well-established norms of Hebrew grammar.

In the first potential passage, Genesis 2:5, Adam is ruled out by context: "there was no *'adam* to till the ground." The point here is not that any *particular* human was missing, but that there were no humans at all to till the ground; the general class of humanity does not yet exist. Adam is not a proper name in this passage. Due to the nature of Hebrew orthography, the other three passages are ambiguous and the definiteness cannot be determined. In each case *'adam* is preceded by an attached preposition that precludes the writing of the definite article. Definiteness at such times is indicated only by the vowel underneath the preposition instead of by the definite article. Vowel markings in the Hebrew text represent a traditional pronunciation and were added to the text no earlier than the fifth century CE, greatly postdating the consonantal text.[14]

The three passages labeled "ambiguous" in appendix 1 (2:20, 3:17, and 3:21) are technically indefinite by that vowel under the preposition (thus allowing for the proper name in theory), but most scholars think this tradition is incorrect. First, all the surrounding occurrences of *'adam* are definite. Second, those who created these vowel markings had inherited a tradition (hundreds of years old by that point) of Adam in the Genesis narrative, which may have influenced their tradition of vowel pointing. If we accept those two arguments, as I do, we cannot read these three occurrences as the proper name Adam.

If not a name, what does *'adam* mean there?

What, then, does *'adam* mean in the text? Other than a proper name, *'adam* represents two things, a class and a member of that class (see

---

14. E. J. Revell, "Masoretes," in *The Anchor Bible Dictionary*, ed. David Noel Freedman (New York: Doubleday, 1992), 4:593–94.

table 1). First and most generally, *ʾadam* can refer to the abstract class of humanity or humankind, in distinction from other animals. Second, more specifically, *ʾadam* can refer to a member of that class, a human or person. Just as *human* and *person* are not gendered terms, neither is *ʾadam*. In this usage, the referent of *ʾadam* could be either male or female. We find *ʾadam* used this way later on in nonnarrative material, such as Leviticus 13:2. Translating *ʾadam* as "anyone," the NIV reads, "When anyone has a swelling or a rash or a shiny spot on their skin that may be a defiling skin disease, they must be brought to Aaron the priest or to one of his sons who is a priest."[15]

Table 1. Representations of *ʾadam*

Most General Level	Abstract class	*ʾadam*/"humanity" or "humankind"
More Specific	A member of that class	*ʾadam*/"a human"
Most Specific Level	A particular member of that class in distinction from the others, i.e., a personal name	*Adam*/"Human"

Terminology indicating the gender of the referent is available both at the human level (i.e., man vs. woman) and at the broad, general level (i.e., male vs. female), *zakar* and *neqēbah*. Both appear together in Genesis 1:27: "So God created humankind [*ʾadam*] in his image, . . . male [*zakar*] and female [*neqēbah*] he created them" (NRSV).[16] Table 2 below shows these paired Hebrew terms.

---

15. New International Version (2011). Note that the translation of masculine singular pronouns in Hebrew (to agree with the grammatically masculine *ʾadam*) results in the nongendered *their* and *they* in English.

16. In other words, God created humanity, both male and female. The NRSV here chooses to pluralize the pronoun, which refers back to *ʾadam*. See note 17.

Table 2. Paired Hebrew terms indicating gender

Paired Hebrew terms	Translational equivalent(s)	Notes
ʾadam (ahDAHM) ʾadamah (uhdahmAH)	A human or person; humankind; Adam (rare) dirt, soil, ground	ʾadamah is formed of the unmarked noun ʾadam with the feminine ending –ah.ª Etymological relationship is uncertain.ᵇ
ʾiyš (eesh) ʾiššah (ishAH)	man woman	The folk etymology in the text takes the form of "woman" to be "man" + feminine ending –ah. In reality, the two terms are unrelated.ᶜ
zakar neqēḇah (nuhkayVAH)	male female	Applied to humans and animals, e.g., Genesis 1:27; 5:2; 6:19; Leviticus 3:1.

a. While ʾadam is a masculine noun, there is no morphological marker to indicate the masculine gender; it is thus the unmarked form.

b. See, for example, the *Word Biblical Commentary* on Genesis 2:7: "Though [ʾadamah] is grammatically the feminine form of [ʾadam] it is doubtful whether there is any etymological connection between the two words. It is sometimes suggested that both terms are derived from [ʾedom] 'red,' the color of man's skin and also the earth. This too seems improbable. Certainly, however, there is a play on the two terms [ʾadam] and [ʾadamah] to emphasize man's relationship to the land. He was created from it; his job is to cultivate it (Genesis 2:5, 15); and on death he returns to it (Genesis 3:19)."

c. Samuel Meier argues that this folk etymology was not possible in earlier stages of the Hebrew language and thus can date no earlier than 1200 BC. See his article "Linguistic Clues on the Date and Canaanite Origin of Genesis 2:23–24," *Catholic Biblical Quarterly* 53/1 (1991).

In Genesis 2–3 ʾadam fluctuates between these two meanings of class versus individual. For the first portion of this narrative, they are one and the same because there is only one member of that class who remains nameless throughout the text. In its very first usage, ʾadam refers to the abstract class of humanity. Genesis 1:27 reads, "Thus God created humankind [ʾadam] in his image; in the image of God did he create it [not him];¹⁷ he created them male and female [zaqar and

---

17. Note that the KJV here reads "him." The pronoun is masculine singular because ʾadam is masculine singular, not because the pronoun refers to the particular man who will come to be known as Adam. Several translations opt for a plural pronoun to avoid misleading on this point, for example, NRSV, NIV, and NET. Fox's *Five Books of Moses* (hereafter FBM) reads "it."

neqēbah]." Humanity, *'adam*, exists as a nameless male and female pair, distinguished only by gender. Note that we are given no substance from which *'adam* is created, and the pair is created simultaneously.

By contrast, Genesis 2:5 informs us that there was no *'adam*, no human, to work the ground (*'adamah*). That ground becomes quite important in 2:7 as God improves upon the personnel situation by shaping or forming *'adam* from the dust of the *'adamah*. In other words, the single *'adam* is formed from the *'adamah*. The word *'adam* appears paired with *'adamah* several times in the text (2:5, 7, 19; 3:17). Some have tried to bring out this linguistic relationship in English by translating with related English words such as "a human from the humus," "a groundling from the ground," or "an earthling from the earth."[18] This indicates that humanity has a special relationship with the ground, but the precise implications are not spelled out, and various ideas and interpretations have been put forth.[19] Note also that the gender of this single *'adam* is not specified, nor is it clear that gender is applicable at this point in the narrative.[20] After the woman is created, we do find gendered terminology indicating that this *'adam* is a male. We also find *'adam* in its second meaning as an individual of the human class, leading translators like Robert Alter and Everett Fox to translate *'adam* consistently as "the human" instead of "the man" (the gendered term) or "Adam."[21]

---

18. See, for example, Phyllis Trible, "Eve and Miriam: From the Margins to the Center," in *Feminist Approaches to the Bible* (Washington, DC: Biblical Archaeology Society, 1995).

19. The ambiguity of *'adam* makes it difficult to know whether this relationship is with all humankind or with the masculine aspect—or with both. That is, does humankind have a special relationship with the ground that other animals do not, but then mankind/males have a further relationship? Is it relevant that after the fall it is the assignment of Groundling to work the ground and the assignment of Life-Giver to give life?

20. Paralleling Greek tradition about the creation of humans, Jewish tradition includes speculation that the lone *'adam* was at first genderless and then split into male and female aspects. This assertion is not well supported by the text, however.

21. See Alter, *Five Books of Moses*; and Fox, *Five Books of Moses*.

Why does the KJV treat *'adam* as a name?

The process of *'adam* becoming the name Adam in Genesis 2–3 involves three stages. First, Adam becomes a proper name relatively quickly beyond Genesis 3 in the Hebrew Bible.[22] Second, that tradition of Adam as a proper name was retrojected into the text of Genesis 2–3 beginning with the early versional translations, which include the Septuagint and targumim. Third, likely under the influence of the versions and theological tradition, early English translations also include the proper name Adam in Genesis 2–3.

The name Adam after Genesis 3

Adam as a proper name appears anarthrously (without the definite marker) and unambiguously as a proper name in Genesis 4:25, "Adam again knew his wife, who bore a son and named him Seth." Again, in Genesis 5:1, Adam is anarthrous and clearly a proper name: "This is the record [*toledot*] of the descendants of Adam."[23] Although both references are clear, they also exist near other usages of *'adam*. Genesis 5:1–3 alludes directly to Genesis 1:26–27 and juxtaposes the proper name with the common noun: "This is the record of the descendants of Adam; when God created *'adam* [or humanity], he created it in the likeness of God. He created them male and female and called them *'adam* [or humanity]. When Adam had lived 130 years, he fathered a son, in his likeness, in his image, and he named him Seth."

Why does the Hebrew Bible convert *'adam* into a proper name so quickly? The narrative logic and asymmetry of Genesis 2–3 certainly suggest it. That is, we have two paired characters in the text, *'iyš* and

---

22. We should recall, though, that the canonical order is not necessarily the chronological order in which the texts were written, which is a much more complicated issue.

23. The *toledot* in Genesis are a long-recognized organizational theme in Genesis, appearing twelve times. All follow the pattern *toledot + proper name*, except for the very first. Genesis 2:4 reads, "These are the generations [*toledot*] of the heavens and the earth when they were created." Esau gets a double mention, and one instance reads "sons of X" instead of "X." Some scholars count the double mention of *toledot Esau* in 36:1 and 36:9 as one occurrence.

ʾiššah, man and woman. The woman receives a name, Eve or Life-Giver, but the man has no name, only a repeated vague descriptor, The Human. His name is a vacuum to be filled, and biblical interpretive tradition loves filling vacuums.

Richard Hess has proposed a linguistic motive for this transition. He examines the range of usage of *ʾadam* in Genesis, from abstract noun *humanity* to semititular use designating one member in particular "the human." He argues that the logical extension of this evolution is a proper name, Adam. That is, "*ʾādām* is a title that reflects a middle point in the continuum from the general usage of *ʾādām* in Genesis 1 to the personal name Adam at the end of Genesis 4."[24]

A partial parallel for this process is found in the name Satan, known today as the personal name of a supernatural figure opposed to Deity. Lexically speaking, it began somewhat as Adam did. First it was a common noun meaning "adversary" or "accuser," sometimes with semititular usage and the definite article. In some texts such as Job and Zechariah, this adversary is a heavenly being, and the noun receives the definite article there, rendering it a title, "The Adversary." Later on, the title gives way to a personal name of an individual, Satan, as is known from Chronicles, the New Testament, and much Second Temple literature outside the Bible. Interpretive tradition then reads this name back into the narratives, just as it does with the name Adam.[25]

The Hebrew Bible does not innovate the use of *ʾadam* as a proper name, as is known from other Semitic sources. The term is found as a personal divine name and the name of a month at Ebla in the third millennium BCE. It may exist in similar usage at Emar, in northern Syria, from the same time period. Usage of Adam as a personal name is unknown between that time period and the writing of Genesis, but

---

24. Richard S. Hess, "Adam," in *Dictionary of the Old Testament: Pentateuch*, ed. T. Desmond Alexander and David W. Baker (Downers Grove, IL: InterVarsity Press, 2003), 19.

25. See, for example, P. L. Day and C. Breytenback, "Satan," in *Dictionary of Deities and Demons in the Bible*, ed. Karel van der Toorn, Bob Becking, and Pieter ven der Horst, 2nd ed. (Leiden: E. J. Brill, 1999).

"the implication is that the earlier into West Semitic texts that one looks, the more likely one is to discover the use of the name Adam."[26]

To summarize stage 1, other sections of the Bible fill the vacuum of the man's name by extending the usage of ʾadam to a personal name, but this was not innovating new usage.

The early versional translations

The third column of the table in appendix 1 represents ancient translations that read ʾadam as a proper name in a given verse. These include the Aramaic targumim (Targum Onqelos, Targum Neofiti, and Targum Pseudo-Jonathan), the Greek Septuagint, and the Latin Vulgate. Being the most certain in date, Jerome's Vulgate comes from circa 400 CE. The Septuagint and targumim probably represent traditions that began as early as 250 BCE for the Septuagint, through the New Testament period, taking final form perhaps as late as the seventh and eighth centuries for Targum Pseudo-Jonathan. These translations, notably, make liberal use of Adam as a proper name. Targums Neofiti and Pseudo-Jonathan are both highly interpretive and expansive, adding Adam even where the Hebrew text lacks ʾadam. Along with New Testament passages such as 1 Timothy 2:13 and Luke 3:38, these early translations clearly attest to early traditions of retrojecting Adam back into the garden narrative.

English translations

The fourth column of the table represents early translations into English from Hebrew, such as Tyndale's Pentateuch and the Coverdale, Bishops', Geneva, and King James Bibles. The KJV was not intended as a new and fresh translation. Rather, the translators were instructed to revise the Bishops' Bible, deviating as necessary in accordance with the Greek and Hebrew.[27] The table shows that the KJV translators were much more expansive in their use of Adam as a proper name than the

---

26. Hess, "Adam," 21.

27. Alister McGrath, *In the Beginning: The Story of the King James Bible and How It Changed a Nation, a Language, and a Culture* (New York: Anchor, 2001), 172–78.

translators of the Bishops' Bible but were only doing what had been done before by Tyndale as well as the Latin Vulgate, Greek Septuagint, and Aramaic targumim nearly fifteen hundred years earlier. The pattern suggests that the KJV translators were generally influenced by the expansiveness of the versions, without slavishly following any one version in particular.

Note, however, the near emptiness of the final column, which shows modern translations that include Adam. Bible translations of the last few decades have largely rejected the interpretive tradition that ignores the rules of Hebrew grammar in including the proper name Adam in Genesis 2–3. The exceptions are the three ambiguous passages where Adam can be inserted without doing violence to the text. However, the translations that do so are largely acting out of respect for tradition and as a concession to their readers who, inheritors of that tradition, expect to see the name Adam there in the text. The conservative evangelical New International Version (or NIV) alone has added it in two more places where it cannot defensibly be on grounds of Hebrew grammar.[28] Most translations that do not include the name Adam at all in Genesis 2–3 begin doing so in Genesis 4:25.[29]

Translating *'adam*

One of the problems of translating *'adam* is that, as we have seen, it means multiple things in the text. An ideal translation captures those meanings while simultaneously reflecting the connections and contrasts that exist in the underlying language. A brief critique of some of these translations will illustrate the challenges.

We have already examined the issues surrounding translation of the phrase "a man from the ground." This translation is problematic because it both suggests an inherently gendered *'adam* and fails to capture the important relationship between *'adam* and *'adamah* that is repeated

---

28. Both the 1984 and 2011 editions insert Adam at 3:20, and the 2011 edition further inserts Adam into 2:25.

29. Using Bibleworks 9, I was able to check more than twenty common and historical English translations.

throughout the text. However, the usage of *man* has something to recommend it. English print can make use of capitalization to indicate different nuances of meaning. One could translate *ʾadam* as "Man" when it refers to humanity and "(the) man" when it refers to the created human individual. This has the advantage of using one English word to represent one Hebrew word while also setting off the different meanings.

However, this usage of *man* creates its own problems later in the passage. When the *ʾadam* is put to sleep and the woman is "constructed" from his side,[30] gendered terminology is introduced by necessity. We need a word for "woman." If we are translating *ʾadam* as "(the) man," it might seem logical that we can simply add the feminine suffix to get *woman*. The two problems with this are that, first, while grammatically masculine, *ʾadam* does not refer to gender. An *ʾadam* is not inherently male in contrast to a female. Second, a noun made of *ʾadam* with the feminine suffix is not grammatically available to us because it has already been used and its meaning is well established in the text as *ʾadamah*, or "ground"!

Thus in Genesis 2:23 the text introduces the gendered terms *ʾiyš* (pronounced "eesh") and *ʾiššah* (pronounced "ish-shah"), meaning man and woman. In doing so the text includes an explicit folk etymology, "She shall be called *ʾiššah*, Woman, because she was taken out of *ʾiyš*, Man." Although *ʾiyš* and *ʾiššah* appear to be a simple case of paired nouns (i.e., an unmarked masculine noun and its gendered counterpart marked with a feminine suffix), *ʾiyš* and *ʾiššah* are unrelated, having completely different roots.[31] Because the terms *man* and *woman* (or *wo-man*) have the same general relationship in English as *ʾiyš* and *ʾiššah* appear to have in Hebrew (i.e., the female noun *woman*/*ʾiššah* includes the male form *man*/*ʾiyš* within it), "man" is a good translation here. Other languages in which *man* and *woman* are unrelated (e.g., French

---

30. The verb used is *banah* "to build, construct."

31. The root of *ʾiyš* is *ʾyš*, but the root of *ʾiššah* is *ʾnš* + the feminine ending *-ah*. When *n* closes a syllable and is followed by certain consonants such as *š*, *n* assimilates and doubles the following consonant instead. Consequently, *ʾnšah* > *ʾiššah*. The masculine counterpart of *ʾiššah* is the rare word *ʾenoš*, which appears to have identical semantic range to *ʾadam*, namely "humankind," "human," and a proper name, Enos (appearing in Genesis 4:26 as the son of Seth, as well as in the Book of Mormon).

homme/femme, German *Mann/Frau*) are often constrained to add a note explaining the Hebrew wordplay or else form a neologism to create a gendered pair.

I have just argued that "man" is a good translation for *'adam* because English capitalization allows it to reflect distinctions between the general and particular usages of *'adam* in the text. I have also argued that "man" is a good translation for *'iyš* because it can capture the folk etymology present in the Hebrew. However, we should still note that it is less than ideal to use *Man* or *man* to translate both *'adam* and *'iyš*, because doing so conflates the different roles the two terms play and can create misreadings. Moreover, the usage of *Man* to mean humankind and *man* or compounds thereof to indicate a person of either gender[32] has largely fallen out of favor. These are not the only issues involved. Caught between the rock of accurate translation and the hard place of felicitous and inoffensive English, translators must make some hard decisions in rendering the text.[33]

What are the implications?

The effects of Adam's linguistic absence from Genesis 2–3 can be debated. Some readers may not see any serious implications at all. But upon reflection, I think there are two. First and very importantly, how we translate (or how the translations we choose to read translate) and how we understand and interpret the text shape our personal beliefs and narratives as well as, for Latter-day Saints, the corporate teachings of the LDS Church. Awareness of how our received traditions have evolved and do not necessarily correspond to the underlying texts in the way we assumed can help provide correctives to those traditions, if necessary.[34] Specifically, Genesis 2–3 is the locus and foundation for

---

32. For example, "If any man . . ." (= person, male or female) or "mailman" (= a male or female mail carrier).

33. See Ben Spackman, "Why Bible Translations Differ: A Guide for the Perplexed," *Religious Educator* 15/1 (2014): 31–66.

34. I suspect that recent updates to the Gospel Topics section of LDS.org—the articles titled "Race and the Priesthood" and "Book of Mormon and DNA Studies," for example—represent examples of examining previously accepted traditions more

many ideas and traditions about women in Judaism and Christianity that led to theology about women, policies about women, and so on, generally not for the better.[35] We cannot separate our understanding of Eve and woman from our understanding of Adam and man in this text. Reevaluating the translation and meaning of one necessitates doing so with the other, but a broader discussion is beyond the scope of this paper.

Second, replacing the name Adam with "the Human" or similar translations as the grammar demands has a generalizing and dehistoricizing effect. It renders the narrative less like a historical account of two specific individuals in the past and more like two archetypal humans known as (the) Human and Life-Giver. From an LDS perspective, as one participant in the Mormon Theology Seminar said, this allows one to read these as "iconic, generic roles to be filled by any individual." This kind of approach may prove fruitful. One recent non-LDS perspective demonstrates how to read this episode archetypally instead of as historical narrative, understanding ʾadam primarily as literary foreshadow of Israel.[36]

Ultimately, the way we translate and the way we read affect beliefs, actions, and policies. Awareness of how our received traditions have evolved and do not necessarily correspond to the underlying texts in the way we assumed helps provide correctives to those traditions, if necessary. Understanding the Hebrew text of Genesis 2–3, and in particular the meaning of the names Adam and Eve therein, may prove useful in responding to problems resulting from overly literal or concordist approaches.

---

closely. See also my post on the power of tradition at http://timesandseasons.org/index.php/2013/06/the-philosophies-of-men-mingled-with-monopoly/.

35. See, for example, Jolene Edmunds Rockwood, "The Redemption of Eve," in *Sisters in Spirit: Mormon Women in Historical and Cultural Perspective*, ed. Maureen Ursenbach Beecher and Lavina Fielding Anderson (Urbana: University of Illinois Press, 1987).

36. Seth D. Postell, *Adam as Israel: Genesis 1–3 as the Introduction to the Torah and Tanakh* (Eugene, OR: Pickwick, 2011).

Appendix 1: Adam in Hebrew and Translations

Ancient translations:[a] LXX,[b] VUL,[c] TO,[d] TN,[e] TPJ[f]

Early modern translations: TYN (1530),[g] COV (1535),[h] BSP (1568),[i] GNV (1560/99),[j] KJV (1611)

Bold indicates the first occurrence of the proper name Adam in that translation.

Passage in Genesis	Definite, indefinite, or ambiguous in Hebrew[k]	Ancient translations with Adam	Early English translations with Adam	Modern English translations with Adam
2:5	indefinite	**TN**		
2:7a	definite	**TO**, TN		
2:7b	definite	TO, TN, (**TPJ**)[l]		
2:8	definite	TN		
2:15	definite	TO, TN	**TYN**	
2:16	definite	**LXX**, TO, TN,[m] TPJ	TYN	
2:18	definite	TO, TN, TPJ		
2:19a	definite	LXX, TO, TN, TPJ, **VUL**	TYN, **KJV**	
2:19b	definite	LXX, TO, TN, TPJ, VUL	TYN, KJV	
2:20a	definite	LXX, TO, TN, TPJ, VUL	TYN, KJV	

a. On each of these ancient translations as well as the English translations, see Bruce M. Metzger, *The Bible in Translation: Ancient and English Versions* (Grand Rapids, MI: Baker Academic, 2001). With the exception of Tyndale's Old Testament (facsimile PDF available online), each of these was examined in Bibleworks 9.

b. Greek Septuagint

c. Latin Vulgate

d. Targum Onqelos

e. Targum Neofiti

f. Targum Pseudo-Jonathan

g. Tyndale's Old Testament

h. Miles Coverdale Bible, 1535. Based on various sources.

i. Bishops' Bible

j. Geneva Bible

k. Some prepositions in Hebrew are attached to the following word, and definiteness is indicated only by the vowel. The notation used in the Masoretic Text to indicate vowels, representing a traditional pronunciation, was not created (as far as we know) until the eighth century CE.

l. The text here is disputed.

m. The primary text violates Aramaic grammar by using a Hebrew definite article, *ha'adam*, whereas the marginal variant reads *'adam*. The Aramaic equivalent of the definite article is a post-positive -*'a*, for example, *'adam'a*. The Comprehensive Aramaic Lexicon Project (http://cal1.cn.huc.edu/) tags both as proper nouns. The reverse happens in 3:12, where the main text reads *'adam* and the variant is *ha'adam*.

Passage in Genesis	Definite, indefinite, or ambiguous in Hebrew[k]	Ancient translations with Adam	Early English translations with Adam	Modern English translations with Adam
2:20b	ambiguous	LXX, TO, TN, TPJ, VUL	TYN, **GNV**, KJV	**ESV, JPS, NAS, NET, NIV**[n]
2:21	definite	LXX, TO, TN, TPJ, VUL	TYN, **BSP**, KJV	
2:22a	definite	LXX, TO, TN, TPJ, VUL	TYN	
2:22b	definite	LXX, TO, TN, TPJ	TYN	
2:23	definite	LXX, TO, TN, TPJ, VUL	TYN, KJV,	
2:25	definite	LXX, TO, TN, TPJ, VUL	TYN	NIV[o]
3:8	definite	LXX, TO, TN, TPJ, VUL	TYN, BSP, **COV**, KJV	
3:9	definite	LXX (x2), TO, TN, TPJ, VUL	TYN, BSP, COV, KJV	
3:12	definite	LXX, TO, TN, TPJ, VUL	TYN, BSP, COV	
3:17	ambiguous	LXX, TO, TN, TPJ, VUL	TYN, BSP, GNV, COV, KJV	**FBM**,[p] ESV, JPS, NIV, NET, NAS
3:20	definite	LXX, TO, TN, TPJ, VUL	TYN, BSP, COV, KJV	NIV
3:21	ambiguous	LXX, TO, TN, TPJ, VUL	TYN, BSP, GNV, COV, KJV	FBM, ESV, JPS, NIV, NET, NAS
3:22	definite	LXX, TN, TPJ, VUL	TYN, COV	
3:24	definite	LXX, TN, VUL	TYN, COV	

n. Both the 1984 and 2011 editions of the New International Version introduce the name Adam here.
o. 2011 edition.
p. Fox, *Five Books of Moses.*

Chaos and Order, Order and Chaos: The Creation Story as the Story of Human Community

James E. Faulconer

Extended prolegomenon

ALONG WITH A NUMBER OF OTHER CONTEMPORARY SCHOLARS, Walter Brueggemann has asked us to remember that God speaks to us in scripture most often through narrative and storytelling rather than systematic theological exposition. Speaking of the first chapters of Genesis, he makes the following observation:

> The story is not explained. It is simply left there with the listening community free to take what can be heard. There is, of course, talk here of sin and evil and death. But it is understated talk. The stakes are too high for reduction to propositions. The story does not want to aid our theologizing. It wants, rather, to catch us in our living. It will permit no escape into theology.[1]

---

1. Walter Brueggemann, *Genesis, Interpretation: A Bible Commentary for Teaching and Preaching* (Atlanta: John Knox Press, 1982), 50.

As Brueggemann says, the story is both concrete and imaginatively open-ended, allowing us the freedom to consider the variety of ways in which present events and those of the story may overlap.[2] Scripture calls for a different kind of reading than what we use for a modern history, philosophy, or theology text.

I will try to take the substance of Brueggemann's warning to heart and read scripture differently than I would read a theology text. And I certainly hope not to read it merely as an aid to theologizing. Nevertheless, I will be doing scriptural theology. But I do so precisely because I think that is a kind of theology that can "catch us in our living" by helping us to read differently than we previously have.

My general interpretive strategy is to make the most sense of the text that I can, as that text presently stands in the canon. I assume that what we have is the product of redaction. Obviously it is also, for most of us, the result of translation and interpretation. Few of us are knowledgeable enough to read the Hebrew text for ourselves. Further, as a cultural artifact and something that we read from within a long history of its influence, the first chapters of Genesis are the result of interpretation for all of us.

But I also assume that the redactors and interpreters who have given us these texts were not blind to what they were doing. In particular, the redactors brought the texts together as they did for some reason. So for me the question is not the historico-critical question, "How did the redactors combine texts to produce the text we have?" but the hermeneutic question, "What meanings do we find in the existing, though redacted, text?" That means that I will read the text literally and typologically. But neither of those terms, particularly not the first, means what our usual thinking about them assumes.

Consider a clue we find in the Bible about how to read biblical texts: Paul speaks of allegory, *allegoria*, in Galatians 4:24, where he uses the story of Hagar and Sarah to make a point about the new covenant and the old covenant. But Paul probably means by *allegory* what we call typology. In a typological reading the reader accepts the literal sense

---

2. Brueggemann, *Genesis*, 4.

of the text but assumes that there is, in addition to the literal meaning, a deeper meaning.

It is important to note, however, that in premodern usage the word *literal* also does not mean what it has come to mean. In other words, it does not mean "free from metaphor, allegory, etc."[3] The word does mean, as it does for us, "depicting a historical event"; but the ancient understanding of history was not our understanding, so it did not cleave apart an account of past events and figurative meaning as we do. As John Walton observes, the first composers and readers of our text "believed that something existed not by virtue of its material properties, *but by virtue of its having a function in an ordered system.*"[4] Ancient history was, therefore, more a matter of giving an account of the order within which things took part than representing the material conditions of an event. In addition, because the historical question had not arisen, resolving the question of a text's historicity was not part of interpreting it. Thus, as Mark Gignilliat says, "the historicity of the OT documents in the pre-critical tradition did not carry the weight that it does in the modern period. To work within this [modern] framework is an imposition of modern sensibilities onto a pre-modern world."[5]

Given these differences between ancient and modern sensibilities, we can say that Paul isn't concerned with the historical accuracy of the text. Surely he understood the story of Hagar and Sarah literally; it is unlikely that he questioned the historical accuracy of the chapters we are reading, though he rarely refers to them (which ought to give us pause). Yet when he does refer to our story, he uses it for its typological significance. For Paul the literal and typological are of a piece, aspects of the same whole. He is concerned with the full sense of the text, including its typological meaning, and not with whether the account is historical.

So I will read the creation story in a way similar to that of Paul: I won't concern myself one way or the other with the historical accuracy

---

3. *Oxford English Dictionary*, s.v. "literal."

4. John H. Walton, *The Lost World of Genesis One: Ancient Cosmology and the Origins Debate* (Downers Grove, IL: InterVarsity, 2009), 26.

5. Mark Gignilliat, "Paul, Allegory, and the Plain Sense of Scripture: Galatians 4:21–31," *Journal of Theological Interpretation* 2 (Spring 2008): 138.

of the text. I will read it literally: by the letter. Perhaps it is more accurate to say that I will give a reading of the plain sense of the text. *Plain* carries less philosophical baggage than *literal*, but as I use these terms neither says anything about historicity. That means, for example, that I won't read the text as if I know that the serpent is Satan, an equivalence established in later texts but not set forth in this narrative or any other part of the canonical Bible. In fact, as part of the narrative, the serpent is a more complicated figure than that straightforward equivalence allows. So I will read this episode as the biblical narrative tells it.

That said, I will not refrain from sometimes reading the creation story with allusions to or pointers from the restoration. Even apart from those references, I will read as a Latter-day Saint. I cannot do otherwise if I take a position in which I recognize the text as canonical.[6] That is not to say that the restoration provides the only or the original meaning of the text. It is to say that the restoration has given us a legitimate reading of the text, even if that legitimacy is based partly on later prophetic inspiration rather than on the original work of the author or the interpretations established in the interpretive traditions.

Long obsessed with the chapters we are reading, I wrote about them in my PhD thesis and have delivered several previous papers on them and published an essay on them in a scholarly journal.[7] But I continue to be obsessed, and I continue to see new things in their story. I will try here to say something new about a theme that has long fascinated me—community, a theme that I've often explored.

My focus will be on the creation story found in Genesis 2–3, which I will treat as a distinct story from the narrative in Genesis 1 or Genesis 1–2:3 (depending on how we understand the first three verses of chapter 2). But I will also read the two stories as related to each other, the first informing my interpretation of the second.

---

6. That is not to say that Latter-day Saints can *only* read as Latter-day Saints. There is no reason to believe that a Latter-day Saint cannot read the Old Testament as a good critical historian rather than as someone taking the text as canonical. Readers of a text do not always read it from the same position within the world.

7. James E. Faulconer, "Adam and Eve—Community: Reading Genesis 2–3," *Journal of Philosophy and Scripture* 1/1 (Fall 2003): 2–16, http://www.philosophyandscripture .org/Issue1-1/James_Faulconer/james_faulconer.html.

Let us start with the overall structure of the story. Several commentators have noted the chiastic structure of Genesis 2–3. Their ways of laying out that chiasmus vary, but they see a chiasmus with its center at Genesis 3:6, Man and Woman's transgression of God's commandment not to eat of the fruit of the tree of knowledge.[8] Taking a cue from Gordon Wenham's way of understanding the chiasmus, I will focus on the movement from outside the garden to inside and then back out again. I'm less concerned, therefore, with the chiastic structure itself than I am with the story's movement and what happens in that movement. I want to think about the changes that occur as the story moves from outside to inside to outside.

As I read the story I will also have in the back of my mind what I take to be part of the original reason for giving this story the shape it presently has: Whatever the origins of the most ancient versions of the text, the story we are looking at was redacted for a sixth-century-BCE audience living in exile in Babylon. Significantly, it situates the Garden of Eden, like Babylon, on the Euphrates (Genesis 2:14), perhaps suggesting thereby that Babylon is a usurper.

I am not a scholar of the ancient Near East, so I am in no position to do anything more than raise a question and make a suggestion. But I wonder whether the serpent in Genesis 3 was meant, among other things, to remind those who heard the story of the Sumerian (and thus Babylonian) god Enlil, the god of air and storms (and breath!) whom humans see as a snake. If so, then one point of the story would be to show that what others take to be a god is, in fact, powerless before the God of Israel.[9] Whether that is the case or not, however, the story certainly refutes the Babylonians' claims about their gods by offering a counternarrative of humankind's relation to Israel's God.

---

8. See, for example, the *HarperCollins Study Bible* (New York: HarperOne, 2006), based on the NSRV; and Gordon J. Wenham, *Vol. 1, Genesis 1–15*, Word Biblical Commentary 50 (Dallas, TX: Word Inc., 1998).

9. According to Wenham, the fact that the text specifically speaks of the serpent as having been created by God (Genesis 3:1) makes that idea suspect: it is unlikely that the text would portray God as having created the god of another nation (*Genesis 1–15*, 72). Since God is the creator of everything, I don't find that argument convincing.

A reading of the garden story as a contestation of Israel's circumstances makes possible a comparison to the situation in which contemporary believers find themselves: in a more or less hospitable world that nevertheless understands human being-in-the-world very differently than the surrounding culture does. In spite of that difference in understanding of what it means to be a human being in the world, the ways of the surrounding culture appear to be similar enough that it is sometimes difficult to tease apart and see the differences between the two. In the sixth century BCE the question was, "How does a believer living in a world that is, in the end, utterly alien though hospitable, retain the relationships with God and other human beings given in the religion of Israel?" Contemporary believers, and certainly not just LDS believers, ask themselves the same question. For me that question takes this form: What does it mean for believers to be together in the world, and is that the fundamental way of being together (whatever *fundamental* might mean here)?

I will read with that question at work in my reading.

The story

Most commentators believe that the first verses of Genesis 2 are the final comment of the first creation story rather than the first comment of the second story. We don't have to reject the scholarly consensus to see what previous readers have seen in the traditional chapter division, which includes verses 1 through 3 in the second story as the link between the two stories of creation. I will read the text in that way, against the grain of contemporary scholarship but along with much of the tradition since the tradition tries to make sense of the redacted text as a whole rather than of the elements that have made up the redaction.

Traditionally our story begins on the Sabbath, with God delighting in the world that he has created. He has brought harmony to physical chaos, and he delights in that harmony. But the earth is as yet barren of cultivated plants, nor does it have someone to cultivate them. Creation remains unfinished.

Significantly, God creates the tiller before he creates the plants to be tilled. In his celebratory delight, he forms an as yet sexually undifferentiated Man. The term *man* specifically designates "male *and* female" in Genesis 1:27, but in Genesis 2:7 it does not yet specify either sex. That is, man is not yet male, because he is singular, and maleness makes sense only in relation to femaleness. Sexual difference is unlike other biological differences. Other differences of kind divide genera and species, but the male/female difference cuts across or within those genera and species. At this point in the story, because Man is alone and has not yet been sexually differentiated, he is not yet fully human.

Imitating what he did in the physical creation, God creates Man from "dust" and God's moist breath. God's breath waters the dust to create Man in the same way that the mist—more accurately a flood or overflow[10]—waters "the whole face of the ground" (Genesis 2:6). Dust is a chaotic nothing or almost nothing from which one must be raised (1 Samuel 2:8; 2 Nephi 1:21). Yet Man's creation from dust suggests also a greater destiny, as Victor Hamilton observes:

> Especially interesting for possible connections with Gen. 2:7 are those passages which speak of an exaltation from dust, with the dust representing pre-royal status (1 K. 16:2), poverty (1 Sam. 2:8; Ps. 113:7), and death (Isa. 26:19; Dan. 12:2). To "be raised from the dust" means to be elevated to royal office, to rise above poverty, to find life. Here man is formed from dust to be in control of a garden. Thus, the emphasis on the dust in Gen. 2:7, far from disagreeing with ch. 1, affirms ch. 1's view of man's regality. He is raised from the dust to reign.[11]

But what does it mean to reign, and over what and how will Man reign?

Initially it appears that Man is to reign over the garden that God creates immediately after Man has been created. It is as if, like an ancient king, God has planted a garden for his pleasure, and he has

---

10. Francis Brown, S. R. Driver, and Charles A. Briggs, *The Enhanced Brown-Driver-Briggs Hebrew and English Lexicon*, electronic ed. (Oak Harbor, WA: Logos Research Systems, 2000), s.v. אך.

11. Victor P. Hamilton, *The Book of Genesis, Chapters 1–17*, New International Commentary on the Old Testament (Grand Rapids, MI: Eerdmans, 1990), 158.

placed within it a gardener to care for it. Someone must "dress and keep it" for the ruler's pleasure. But there are indications that Man is to be more than just the gardener appointed to maintain the harmony and beauty of the royal garden. Perhaps the most important indication is that Man is created before rather than after the garden is planted. Man is "a living soul" (Genesis 2:7), a breathing being rather than one without breath, in Man's case the breath of God.[12] As such he has an importance in the world superior to the plants of the garden, which are without breath. He comes before them.

We see a further suggestion of Man's status as more than servant in the word translated "till" (Genesis 2:5: "There was not a man to till the ground"). That word is more often used of worship, as in Deuteronomy 4:19, and it is especially used of the Levites' duties in the tabernacle (Numbers 3:7–8; 8:26; 18:5–6). In the same vein, Gregory Beale notes that the Hebrew words translated "dress and keep" in the King James translation

> can easily be, and usually are, translated "serve and guard." When these two words occur together later in the OT, without exception they have this meaning and refer either to Israelites "serving and guarding/obeying" God's word (about 10 times) or, more often, to priests who "serve" God in the temple and "guard" the temple from unclean things entering it (Num 3:7–8; 8:25–26; 18:5–6; 1 Chr 23:32; Ezek 44:14).[13]

---

12. R. Laird Harris, Gleason L. Archer Jr., and Bruce K. Waltke, *Theological Wordbook of the Old Testament*, electronic ed. (Chicago: Moody, 1999), 588, s.v. נֶפֶשׁ.

13. The passage from which this shorter quotation is extracted is instructive:

> First, the temple later in the OT was the unique place of God's presence, where Israel had to go to experience that presence. Israel's temple was the place where the priest experienced God's unique presence, and Eden was the place where Adam walked and talked with God. The same Hebrew verbal form (*hithpael*), *hithallek*, used for God's "walking back and forth" in the Garden (Gen 3:8), also describes God's presence in the tabernacle (Lev 26:12; Deut 23:14 [15]; 2 Sam 7:6–7).

Tilling, serving, and guarding are the work of Levite priests. Man is to be God's priest in the garden temple, to serve him there and to guard against any unclean thing entering that sacred space and disrupting its harmony. In the first creation story, God brought order to chaos. In the second, Man is created to guard against chaos. In particular, because the tree of life and the tree of knowledge of good and evil are the only plants specifically named, it appears that Man is to dress and guard them from disorder.

But Man is commanded not to eat of the second tree. Part of his duty as guard is to guard the tree of knowledge from himself. He is implicitly noted as a potential source of disorder from the beginning. As gardener, he may share in the fruit of the garden, even in some of the best, but the fruit of the tree of knowledge is reserved, one might assume, for the King.

Whatever it means for this to be the tree of knowledge of good and evil, the knowledge it imparts cannot be just the ability to discern between right and wrong. If it were, it would be impossible to later hold Man and Woman responsible for disobeying the injunction against eating the fruit. They cannot be punished for choosing wrongly if they

---

Second, Gen 2:15 says God placed Adam in the Garden "to cultivate it and to keep it." The two Hebrew words for "cultivate and keep" (respectively, ʿābad and shāmar) can easily be, and usually are, translated "serve and guard." When these two words occur together later in the OT, without exception they have this meaning and refer either to Israelites "serving and guarding/obeying" God's word (about 10 times) or, more often, to priests who "serve" God in the temple and "guard" the temple from unclean things entering it (Num 3:7–8; 8:25–26; 18:5–6; 1 Chr 23:32; Ezek 44:14). (Gregory K. Beale, "Eden, the Temple, and the Church's Mission in the New Creation," *Journal of the Evangelical Theological Society* 48/1 [March 2005]: 7–8.)

This comparison of the garden to the tabernacle or temple is not uncommon. For example, Sailhamer says that "the description of God's placing man in the garden … bears strong resemblance to the later establishment of the priesthood for the tabernacle and the temple" (John H. Sailhamer, "Genesis," in *The Expositor's Bible Commentary, Volume 2: Genesis, Exodus, Leviticus, Numbers,* ed. Frank E. Gaebelein [Grand Rapids, MI: Zondervan, 1990], 43). And Wenham notes that, like the tabernacle, the garden faces east (*Genesis 1–15*, 86).

do not know the difference between right and wrong at all. As is easily imaginable, the question of what kind of knowledge was provided by the forbidden fruit has been much discussed over the last several millennia. The conclusions vary, but I find convincing the arguments of W. M. Clark and others, such as Umberto Cassuto, that the wisdom given is the divine ability to act autonomously, not just the ability to discriminate right from wrong.[14]

In the first story of creation, we were told that sexually differentiated human beings (that is, male-female "man," Genesis 1:27) are made in the image of God. On that understanding they are like the statues that ancient Near Eastern kings set up in their kingdom to assert their rule even where they were not present.[15] In the story of the garden, however, the as yet sexually undifferentiated Man is not yet a representative of the King's presence. Even if a different future is intimated early in the story, in the beginning he is only a servant, and to servants some things—in Man's case the fruit of the tree of knowledge of good and evil—are forbidden.

However, this gardener cannot do his work of serving God and guarding the garden as long as he remains unique, sexually undifferentiated. He is not yet fully in the image of God. As yet creation is not fully ordered; it remains chaotic. As yet neither male nor female, Man can neither dress nor keep the garden.

Though he finds himself in the garden temple, Man cannot be God's priest. God says that this is not good (Genesis 2:18), using a Hebrew emphatic negative. Then he teaches Man about his lack by having him compare himself to "every living creature" (Genesis 2:19). That comparison reveals Man's uniqueness: he alone is alone. Because he is asexual, no other creature is the helper in the garden who is appropriate for him. But God will take care of that problem by creating a help meet for him.

---

14. W. M. Clark, "A Legal Background to the Yahwist's Use of 'Good' and 'Evil' in Gen 2–3," *Journal of Biblical Literature* 88 (1969): 266–78; and Umberto Cassuto, *A Commentary on the Book of Genesis: Part I, from Adam to Noah, Genesis I–VI 8*, trans. Israel Abrahams (Jerusalem: Magnes, 1961).

15. Brueggemann, *Genesis*, 32.

The Hebrew phrase translated "help meet" literally means "helper like [and] opposite him."[16] The point appears to be that the new creature will be like but not identical to Man. This relationship of both sameness and difference that characterizes sexual difference is essential to creation. Without it, God has said, the world is emphatically not good. It remains chaotic. Creation is incomplete without sexual difference. The problem is that with sexual difference there is always a possible new source of chaos.

As we will see, in this story the source *and* resolution of chaos are the same: human, sexually differentiated being. From the beginning of the garden, when it was planted as part of creation's Sabbath, it contained chaos that came from outside the garden, namely, Man's chaos of lack and absence. That is the implicit chaos of being neuter and singular and, so, unable either to serve God or to protect the garden from impurity. The answer to that chaos is sexual difference within the garden. But as those who already know this story, we know that the answer is also going to be a problem.

In sum: God expressed his Sabbath rest by creating Man and planting the garden of paradise. But by giving singular Man the duty of the gardener, God reintroduced chaos to creation. The irony, of course, is that the resolution of this particular chaos, namely, the resolution of Man's lack by the creation of sexual differentiation, will introduce chaos again. Chaos and order are inextricably entwined. Each creation is an ordering of chaos, but each ordering of chaos brings new potential for chaos, and there is no end to that entwined relationship. In fact, creation *is* that entwinement. Traditionally, religions of "the Book" have seen an eventual end to the continuation of creation, an ultimate overcoming of chaos with perfect harmony in one kind or another of an eschatology. But this story, at least, envisions no such end.

Genesis teaches us, then, that for Man to have a companion—in other words, for there to be both male and female—neuter Man must be wounded by having a rib removed, anticipating the wound of childbirth that Eve will later be given (Genesis 3:16). By wounding asexual Man, God makes—literally builds—Woman and in doing so creates

---

16. Wenham, *Genesis 1–15*, 68.

not one new being but two. Now we have not only Woman but also Man in a sexual sense. The sexually differentiated couple, the new Man and the new Woman, come into being together as the first human beings, and they come into being via the wounding of a singular, asexual Man, a sexually undifferentiated human being. The chaos of the wound makes possible the harmony of the Man-Woman couple. They are now—almost—full human beings.

Before he entered into the deep sleep from which a new creation would emerge, neuter Man recognized that he lacked something. But he seemed not to understand what he lacked. Now, in a song of joy, the newly reborn Man recognizes what had been missing: Woman. "This one (zō'ṯ) at last is bone of my bone and flesh of my flesh [a standard kinship formula]; this one (zō'ṯ) shall be called woman ('iššâ) because this one (zō'ṯ) has been taken from man ('îš).[17] Man has found the one he could not find among the animals. "This one" is the helper appropriate to him. As one flesh, one heart, one soul,[18] the needed gardener has come into being in this couple. As a couple they are presumably ready to serve in the garden and to guard it against impurity.

But their service and guarding will turn out to mean more than serving and guarding. In fact, it will eventually mean that they can no longer serve as priest and priestess in the Edenic temple, though it will also mean the representation, the imaging, of God. We find the possibility of the commonality and coming together of human community (and human being with God) in human identity as sexually differenced. However, the difference that makes community possible is also the possible source of the community's disruption, chaos. Living in the tension of that sameness and difference is what it means to be kin, to be companions in the bone and flesh. That similarity and difference is what is necessary for one's being able not only to serve but to represent or image another.

---

17. Translation from John J. Scullion, "Genesis, the Narrative of," in *The Anchor Bible Dictionary*, ed. David Noel Freedman (New York: Doubleday, 1992), 2:945.

18. Scriptures such as Psalm 84:2 suggest that *heart, flesh,* and *soul* are different ways of speaking of the same thing, the whole of human being.

The couple is the real entity, a whole. Each member of the couple represents not only himself or herself but the couple as a whole. As part of the couple, each person represents all of humanity, though humanity is disrupted by a sexual difference that cannot be incorporated into its individual members. That differenced unity, which is the ground for human representation, is similar to the way in which the couple is related to God: each is like God and yet not like him at all. This relation of sameness and difference is what will eventually make it possible for the First Couple to go beyond merely serving God to representing him.

With the creation of Woman, human beings, as a sexually differentiated couple of one bone and one flesh, can now serve God and guard the garden. They can begin to represent the King in his garden. But all who know the story know that this first representation of the King's gardeners in the King's garden will reintroduce chaos and put the couple outside the garden where, not without irony, they will finally be in the image of God and will be expected to serve him.

This irony is foreshadowed by the redactor's comment in Genesis 2:24: "Therefore shall a man leave his father and his mother, and shall cleave unto his wife." In an earlier essay I pointed out the hermeneutic importance of this seemingly parenthetical note:

> Man and Woman will be forced to leave their father and mother—in this case God—and cleave to each other: in order to be human Man and Woman must leave the divine communion of paradise to live in community with others. In other words, they must die; they must live in history. . . . It is not simply that Man and Woman have the option of remaining immortally in the garden in ignorance or leaving with knowledge to die. But—if their lives are to be meaningful, . . . if they are to escape the emphatic negative with which God has judged the situation of one alone, in other words, if they are to be human—they must live in community and they must do so estranged from God.[19]

---

19. Faulconer, "Adam and Eve," 16.

At the end of chapter 2 (a division created millennia after the text came into being) the redactor is explicit about the nature of ongoing creation: it requires ongoing separation and union, a separation and union revolving around sexual difference. We see in chapter 2 the beginning, but only the beginning, of human community. Full human community, the verse suggests, is as yet something to continue to anticipate.

I believe that this necessity of ongoing separation and union, chaos and harmony, drives the rapid turn of the story from "They were naked and not ashamed" (Genesis 2:25) to "Behold, the man has become as one of us" (Genesis 3:22) and to the expulsion of Adam and Eve from the garden. The translation "not ashamed" is problematic because the Hebrew word that the phrase translates doesn't carry the sense of guilt that we associate with shame. "Unabashed" might be a better translation.[20] In any case, the transition from unabashed nakedness to being like God requires the story of separation and union that we find in chapter 3.

The first thing to notice about Genesis 3:1 is that, though God has been very much a part of every step of the story so far, now he is suddenly absent. On my reading, in which the original Man is unable to be the gardener, the creation of the Edenic couple has made it possible for the King to leave his garden in the gardeners' care. But left to their care in the King's absence, the garden is quickly defiled: a snake enters in. Man and Woman have not been at their task of guarding the garden against defilement. But not only has God disappeared, perhaps so has Man. Man and Woman are, at the moment of Genesis 3:1, not yet a couple. They are in some sense individuals, and the serpent will appeal to that individuality.

Like God, the serpent has a wisdom. He is described as "crafty" or "shrewd," which translates a word that is mostly a positive trait in the Old Testament, the ability to know what to do. He is the shrewdest of any living nonhuman creature. But for readers familiar with the eating prohibitions of Leviticus 11, the serpent is also one of the unclean animals, perhaps one of the most unclean, given the ordering of the Leviticus text.

---

20. Wenham, *Genesis 1–15*, 71. See Judges 3:25 and 2 Kings 2:17 for uses of the Hebrew root (*svb*) that do not carry the connotation of guilt.

Chaos has entered the garden from outside, and the story as a whole turns on that entry, the entry of a kind of wisdom other than godly wisdom. In Genesis 3:1 the text marks the turn by making perhaps the most obvious and most important wordplay of the story, for the Hebrew term translated "naked" (*arom*) in Genesis 2:25 is very much like the word translated "subtil" or "shrewd" (*arum*) here. As we all know, the serpent's wisdom is that of rhetoric and, as Brueggemann points out, theology. The snake replaces obedience to God's wisdom with critical reflection and theological parsing.[21] He has wisdom, the wisdom that we continue to prize, but he doesn't have the wisdom of God, the "knowledge of good and evil."

Odd as that sounds, it is important to recognize that the serpent assumes, correctly, that divine wisdom means choosing between good and evil without any appeal to authority, such as revelation. But in his shrewdness the serpent confuses that divine wisdom with his analytic wisdom of reflection, critique, and parsing, making the latter at least the same as the former, if not superior. Lacking God's wisdom, his ability simply to know the good from the evil, the serpent conflates that wisdom with his own shrewdness, his know-how, his wisdom for getting things done by analysis. He is modern well before his time.

Though the serpent never contradicts what God has said, he skeptically suggests that God has commanded something different than he in fact did: perhaps, his question suggests, God forbade Man and Woman from eating from *any* tree rather than forbidding only the fruit of the tree of knowledge of good and evil. Notice, too, that the serpent never tells Woman to eat the fruit of the tree. He makes his skeptical suggestions and allows her to choose. And though (in Genesis 3:4) he contradicts God's declaration that those who eat the forbidden fruit would die (Genesis 2:17), what the snake says is almost precisely what the text later tells us happened: Man and Woman do not die when they eat the fruit; instead their eyes are opened (Genesis 3:7), and they become like God and those with him (Genesis 3:22). Using the truth against God, the serpent suggests that God is trying to keep human beings from becoming like him, that the only way to become

---

21. Brueggemann, *Genesis*, 47–48.

like God is to defy him. Misunderstanding divine wisdom, the serpent assumes that he knows what God's wisdom is, and therefore he suggests to Woman that to become like God is to exercise autonomous will. Autonomy is confused with individual will. Once again, the serpent says what is true but says it falsely, for he implies that becoming like God means stepping out of the harmony of Man-Woman and God in the garden to become an individual will.

But the Woman is no simpleton merely following the lead of a shrewd tempter. She shows what appears to be at least the beginning of rhetorical or legal skill even before she eats the fruit. She expands the commandment that had been given, putting a hedge about the commandment by adding "neither shall ye touch it" (Genesis 3:3). She has designed to protect herself from violating God's prohibition. Yet she also responds to the serpent's suggestion that God is keeping something from her by seeing the tree in a new way. It is no longer forbidden, but has become "good for food, and . . . pleasant to the eyes, and a tree to be desired to make one wise" (Genesis 3:6), and this new way of seeing makes the hedge ineffective.

The wording of Genesis 3:6 suggests that what Woman does is already comparable to what God has done. As sovereign Creator, at each stage of creation, he "saw that it was good." Now Woman looks at the fruit of the tree and "sees that it is good." The Hebrew is the same in each case. Thus, even before Woman eats the fruit, she has begun to act in a godlike way, assuming the position of a sovereign, someone autonomous, over whom no one else has authority. Then she eats and shares the fruit with Man so that he, too, can be an individual. What was created as a differenced unity intended to be one flesh has become two individuals.

As we look at Genesis 3:6, it is important to note that the story isn't that of simple rebellion against God's authority. Rather, it is "a quest for wisdom and 'the good' apart from God's provision."[22] It is the attempt to find the good individually and autonomously. But that quest is a letdown. As the wordplay of Genesis 2:25 and 3:1 already predicted, through the serpent's shrewdness Man and Woman go from

---

22. Sailhamer, "Genesis," 52.

being unknowingly naked to knowing that they are naked. In probably a variety of ways, they come to know that they are embodied beings. The text doesn't tell us that they were ashamed of that embodiment, only that they knew it needed covering. They have discovered bodily need. As their fig-leaf garments show, they have also discovered that as autonomous beings they cannot meet their need in any satisfactory way.

Left to serve in the garden and to protect it from defilement, Man and Woman have allowed it to be defiled. They have introduced chaos. And chaos has defiled not only the garden but them. And they cannot remedy their defilement. God must step in to re-create the world and restore order, though as in each previous case, the order will be a new order, not merely a return to the old.

When God first encounters Man and Woman, they are hiding for fear (the same emotion that in other places is the awe of God's presence, e.g., Psalm 110:10). Perhaps they are ashamed of their naked bodies, but that isn't what the text says. It says they are afraid of God because they know they are naked. Rather than understanding their response to their nakedness as shame, perhaps we should understand it as a fear induced by the absence of the priestly clothing they now know they should wear if they are to serve God and guard his temple. Or perhaps it is simply awe: previously the gardeners had known God but appear not to have been in awe of him. Now that they have his wisdom, they are awestruck in his presence.

Whatever the cause of Man and Woman's fear, in that fear they experience the distance between themselves and God, distance created by eating the fruit. But eating it has also put distance between themselves, as Man's attempt to blame Woman (Genesis 3:12) and her attempt to blame the serpent (Genesis 3:13) show. They have acted in autonomy and now find themselves in the separation and chaos of that autonomy.

At the end of chapter 2, as Brueggemann notes, the story was one of trust and obedience. Now it has become what at first reading appears to be a story of crime and punishment.[23] But it is less straightforwardly

---

23. Brueggemann, *Genesis*, 48.

that than we might assume. For, though God's response to their fear and blaming is to curse the serpent,[24] when he turns to Man and Woman his language has neither the form nor the wording of curses. Though centuries of interpretation have dimmed the possibility of reading these pronouncements as anything other than punishment, I think it makes sense to read them instead as sentences of grace. God's graciousness is not just what we see first in Genesis 3:21 with God's gift of clothing, but what we see in Genesis 3:16: "I will greatly multiply thy sorrow and thy conception; in sorrow thou shalt bring forth children."[25] That doesn't sound like a gift, but I argue that it is.

Equally, the response to Man is to curse the earth "for thy sake," according to the King James translators," but simply "because of you" for most modern translators. But we can see the reasoning behind the King James translation: if the earth is cursed because of Man, then unless this is simply an injustice to the earth, it is cursed *for* human beings. He will eat the fruit of the earth in sorrow, the same word in both Hebrew and English that he used to describe the consequences of Woman's transgression. The Hebrew word (*'iṣṣābhōn*) suggests physical pain as much as it does sorrow.[26] Both Man and Woman learn that to be human with the wisdom needed to discriminate between good and evil on one's own means work and that work means suffering. That is God's grace to them: he gives them their full humanity in work and pain, which is also their imitation of Divinity. The result of the story, as God tells us, is that the couple has come to be "as one of us" (Genesis 3:22). In other words, Adam and Eve learn that divine wisdom comes only in a relation between individuals who are both together and separated in creating, rather than merely autonomous.

---

24. The wordplay continues, for the serpent who had been crafty (*arum*) is now cursed (*arur*).

25. Brueggemann, *Genesis*, 49.

26. See Brown, Driver, and Briggs, *Hebrew and English Lexicon*, s.v. עִצָּבֹון. Cassuto suggests that there is a wordplay here on the Hebrew word for tree: "it was with respect to עֵץ *ēṣ* [tree] that man and woman sinned, and it was with עֶצֶב *eṣebh* ('pain') and עִצָּבֹון *'iṣṣābhōn* ('toil, suffering') that they were punished" (Cassuto, *Commentary on the Book of Genesis*, 165).

The result of eating the fruit is chaos. But that chaos is the chaos within which human community arises, and it is the chaos resulting from God's pleasure in creation. Genesis 3:16 says that Woman's urges are toward Man. But Genesis 3:20 suggests that Man is also turned toward her as *her* creation: she was taken out of wounded, sexually undifferentiated Man, but Adam is now who he is as a human being through what wounded Woman has done. He calls her Eve because "she was the mother of *all* living" (Genesis 3:20, emphasis added)—including him.

Just as sexually undifferentiated Man was wounded in order for the human couple, Man and Woman, to exist, humanity's existence presumes Eve's wound. At the beginning of creation is a wound, chaos. Comparably, at the beginning of all full human being is Eve's wound. The result of these two wounds is Adam and Eve's laboring pain as persons living together in community: the constant undoing and redoing and undoing of the wound of chaos.

It is impossible not to recognize that for millennia the Genesis story, among other uses, has been used to explain and justify the subordination of women to men. I do not see this story as a story that intends to call that subordination into question—at least partly because the question had not yet arisen. But because it speaks from outside the realm of that question, neither do I think that the story must or even ought to be read as supporting that traditional subordination. We can read the text against that particular grain. When we do, I believe that, instead, we see this pericope even more fully as a story about the origin of human community as a relation of tension between sameness and difference, between harmony and chaos.

Conclusion

The community begins in Sabbath harmony outside the garden, in a singular, unsexed Man created ostensibly to represent his maker. He is placed inside the garden not only to represent God but also to serve him and to guard the garden. All three (representation, priesthood service, and guarding against defilement) turn out to require the sexing of human being, the relation of male and female and the need to leave father and mother and cling to one's mate. But the harmony of the garden watched over by Man and Woman cannot last. If Man and Woman are to represent God, they will need not only the wisdom of gardeners—they will also need God's wisdom, a wisdom presumably acquired in watching and guarding his creation through work and without avoiding suffering.

So the story turns out to be a story about moving outside the garden, leaving the presence of God in order to live with one another in divinely given life. But the story of divine life is about the unavoidable work and pain of human existence together. It reminds us that inevitable chaos makes the labor of human existence in community continually necessary. As human beings we are not just Man, nor are we merely Man and Woman. We are Adam and Eve, individuals with the wisdom of God's relational, sexually differenced existence rather than the critical reflection and theological parsing of the serpent's individual autonomy. We live with the consequences of our divine existence in ongoing tension of chaos and creation that defines the human and godly world.

Creation, Localism, and Appetite in the Garden World of Wendell Berry

Rosalynde Welch

A SENSE OF PLACE IS CENTRAL TO THE WORK OF FIDELITY. This is the contention of Walter Brueggemann in his book *The Land*, and it is the germ of an emergent Christian localism.[1] An energetic, unwieldy coalition of social, economic, and ideological impulses, localism in its various forms settles around a thick notion of place. In the special sense invoked here, *place* implies the rooted, particular meanings and conditions and communities native to any given vicinity, over and against an abstract notion of empty, neutral space. A Christian localism, then, seeks and celebrates thick places in its sacred texts, its particular histories, and its native ways of life.

The marriage of Christianity and localism is not conceptually inevitable: after all, "foxes have holes, and birds have nests, but the Son of Man has nowhere to lay his head" (Luke 9:58).[2] There has always been a universalizing and expansive moment in the Christian gospel that militates against rooted particularism. To the extent that a Christian localist outlook coheres, though, it does so around two projects.

---

1. Walter Brueggemann, *The Land: Place as Gift, Promise, and Challenge in Biblical Faith* (Minneapolis: Fortress, 2002).

2. Robert Alter, *The Five Books of Moses: A Translation with Commentary* (New York: W. W. Norton, 2004). Alter's translation is used throughout.

The first is a critique of the "dominion" language in Genesis 1, or of the triumphalist interpretation thereof that has been marshalled to authorize human exploitation of the natural world and, indeed mistakenly, to dualize "man" and "nature."[3]

The second project of Christian localism, and its best gift to the larger movement, is its effort to recover "the art of being creatures."[4] Biblical teachings on creation lay out a creaturely economy in which humanity is placed—that is, charged with a given vocation, bound with given promises, and yoked among given creatures whose natures also unfold within this economy. A paradigmatic instance of this is the prominence of soil in the Eden narrative: soil mingles with the life and death of every creature living from, on, and in it, minutely specific to place. Eden's soil is the substrate of the human placed therein, and this soil mediates most of the promises and relationships that define the human's vocation. This emphasis on creatureliness throws into relief human dependence and interdependence, as God's dust and God's wind in a world not of our making and scarce of our knowing.

This last point, the creaturely limits of human knowledge, is especially salient to the larger localist movement. Localism implies social and economic formations, yes, but beyond that it suggests an epistemology, a way of knowing and making knowledge. The insight begins with a welcome reminder that local stores of knowledge are worth attending to, and makes the further point that *all knowledge is local*. All knowledge is produced within communities, often imagined communities, and organized around local interests and meanings and hierarchies. As Brueggemann puts it, "There are no meanings apart from roots."[5] Various trajectories of critical theory arrived at the social construction of knowledge long before Christian localism did, of course, but a Christian perspective redirects the idea away from

---

3. See Lynn White Jr., "The Historical Roots of Our Ecologic Crisis," in *Western Man and Environmental Ethics: Attitudes toward Nature and Technology*, ed. Ian G. Barbour (Reading, MA: Addison-Wesley, 1973), 18–30.

4. Norman Wirzba, "The Art of Being a Creature," in *The Gift of Creation: Images from Scripture and Earth* (Sikeston, MO: Acclaim Press, 2009).

5. Brueggemann, *Land*, 4.

nihilism and toward humility, mystery, a willingness to rest in uncertainty and unfolding.

As a social movement, localism did not germinate in the church, but Christianity is central to the thought of localism's visionary poet-prophet, Wendell Berry, and the overtly biblical localism that has appeared in the past decade owes much to Berry's impressive corpus of poetry, fiction, and cultural criticism amassed over five decades and counting. Berry directly addresses biblical creation narratives in his essay "God and Country." If his reading of the Eden narrative seems predictable, that is only because it has been so widely adopted since it was written in 1988. He argues that Adam and Eve were not given the earth as entitlement, but as gift and obligation. His watchwords are "service, stewardship, and the responsible care of property belonging to another," and he quotes Hugh Nibley's observation that "man's dominion is a call to service, not a license to exterminate."[6] Berry invokes the ancient law of usufruct, the right to temporarily enjoy the fruits of land belonging to another so long as the property remains undamaged. It's a useful discussion, but uncharacteristically for Berry, it avoids the hard questions, both textual and ecological. Does Eve's bite from the fruit violate the law of usufruct? It seems not. Where, then, is the sin? Are humans permitted to alter the appearance or function of landscape or organism for purely aesthetic reasons, if it seems to leave the ecosystem unharmed? What about special attempts to protect landscapes that particularly appeal to humans instead of those that do not, as in the national park system? What constitutes "damage" to the land, since any change to an ecosystem will harm some species and benefit others? Whose welfare prevails?

The nature of this damage is the theme taken up in Berry's poem of the same name; this is the text I intend to bring into dialogue with Genesis 2–3. The poem makes no specific reference to the Eden tale, but its themes are deeply related, and in my view "Damage" is Berry's more interesting treatment of our text. The poem is an account of Berry's attempt to convert a wooded, waterless hillside into a pasture by

---

6. Wendell Berry, "God and Country," in *What Are People For? Essays* (Berkeley: North Point Press, 1990), 99.

clearing trees and creating a pond. The hillside is his Eden, given to him in its particular form, magnificently indifferent to his cattle's need for water and grass. Berry wants to alter it. He hires a man with a bulldozer to clear trees and dig earth; water seeps into the gash; Berry reseeds the hillside "to heal the exposed ground." His desire and his self-deception allow him to believe that grass and clover can mitigate the erosive effects of the bulldozer. After a "wet fall,"

> [t]he ground grew heavy with water, and soft.
> The earthwork slumped; a large slice of the woods floor on the upper side slipped down into the pond.

His Eden falls. He convicts himself: the trouble is "too much power, too little / knowledge. The fault was mine." The poem concludes in reflection on the question of environmental damage: as both nature poet and farmer, Berry is forced by these dual roles to exploit his subject for his livelihood:

> If I have damaged my subject, then I have damaged my art. What aspired to be whole has met damage face to face, and has come away wounded....

> To lose the scar of knowledge is to renew the wound.[7]

Soil, trees, creature, appetite, technology, fall, sin: these are the load-bearing themes of the Genesis narrative as well, and the two texts suggest themselves as interlocutors.

Beyond thematic kinship, the texts share a particular blurriness, a thematic uncertainty at the center of the drama. For Berry, the blind spot occurs at the nexus of technology and appetite: the bulldozer is the proximate cause of the scarred hillside; Berry's own appetite for pasture is the ultimate cause—or so it would seem. But the poem's concluding stanzas spin off into a series of misdirections: the real cause is the degradation of local culture, or the real cause is the machine's artificial

---

7. Berry, "Damage," in *What Are People For?*, 5–7.

multiplication of human power, or the real cause is confusion of tools with weapons. In the end, the poem hesitates doubtfully between these undertheorized alternatives, leaving uncertain the nature of the collusion between human technology and human appetite in Berry's fallen Eden.

For its part, the Genesis narrative harbors a tree-shaped textual gap of its own, namely, the nature of the tree of knowledge and the character of the knowledge it confers. At the center of Yahweh's garden stands what Ellen Davis has called "The Tree of Ambiguous Wisdom"; as Davis observes, the narrative itself seems uninterested in limning the tree or guiding the reader's interpretive response.[8] What sort of knowledge does it bestow on the woman who eats? Esoteric wisdom, sexual knowledge, moral law, consilient knowledge, as E. O. Wilson terms the demystifying knowledge products of science? On this matter the text is silent, yet the reader's understanding of the events that follow—the rupture and dislocation, the introduction of technology, the changes in human nature and vocation—depends on the meaning of the tree of knowledge.

The structuring design of this paper, and the burden of its argument, is that the two texts inform one another, each opening a view into the particular blind spot of the other. Where Genesis is silent on the nature of knowledge, "Damage" draws out the local, experiential nature of the knowledge conferred by fallen earth. Where "Damage" obscures the intersection of human appetite and technology, Genesis observes the instrumentalizing collusion between consumption and construction.

To the latter first. Berry's "Damage" begins with hunger: his cattle's hunger for grass, his own hunger for cattle. A pasture is wanted, but on his steep hillside no pasture is given. What is given—timber, soil, slope—is of no use for pasturing cattle. Berry thus finds himself in the position of the woman in Eden: surrounded by the fruits of a garden freely given, but filled with appetite only for what is not. For Eve, appetite obscures the intrinsic nature of the desired object and projects

---

8. Ellen Davis, *Scripture, Culture, and Agriculture: An Agrarian Reading of the Bible* (Cambridge: Cambridge University Press, 2009), 30–31.

instead a scrim of imagined gratification: "And the woman saw that the tree was good *for eating* and that it was lust *to the eyes* and the tree was lovely *to look at,* and she took of its fruit and ate" (Genesis 3:6, emphasis added). The tree of knowledge is itself a creature of Yahweh, possessing intrinsic qualities and vocation independent of human appetite, but the woman sees it only through a lens of desire and imagined consumption: the tree is not good, but good for eating; not lovely, but lovely to look at.

As it was for Eve, so it must have been for Berry, gazing at his dry wooded hillside and seeing only water for drinking and clover for eating. Yet the poem is silent on Berry's own hunger for pasture, his original whim. It falls to Genesis to point up the two farmers' hungry self-absorption, their assumption that the world is conveniently available. Blinded by appetite, they fail to grasp the wisdom of Thoreau: "This curious world we inhabit is more wonderful than convenient; more beautiful than it is useful; it is more to be admired and enjoyed than used."[9]

The bracing lesson implicit in Eve's experience, namely, that the world exists in its own right and independent of human purposes, is braided through the length of the Old Testament because it is inscribed in ancient Israel's most elemental identity, its relationship to land. Of the Israelite practice of land sabbath, Berry observes, "Looking at their fallowed fields, the people are to be reminded that the land is theirs only by gift; it exists in its own right, and does not begin or end with any human purpose."[10] Even when understood, the lesson is not easy to live. Eve's hungry gaze beams from all human eyes. The remedy is to re-*place*: that is, to reroot ourselves in thick place, and to replace gaze with contemplation. In the words of George Grant, contemplation is the *place*-ing of the eye, a "wondering, marveling, being amazed or astonished, beyond all bargains and conveniences."[11]

---

9. Henry David Thoreau, 1837 Harvard commencement speech, quoted in Fritz Oehlschlaeger, *The Achievement of Wendell Berry: The Hard History of Love* (Lexington, KY: University Press of Kentucky, 2011), 38–39.

10. Wendell Berry, *The Gift of Good Land: Further Essays Cultural and Agricultural* (Berkeley: North Point, 1981), 271.

11. George Grant, quoted in David L. Schindler, *Ordering Love: Liberal Societies and the Memory of God* (Grand Rapids, MI: Eerdmans, 2011), 279.

If "Damage" attends too little to the culpability of Berry's own appetite for pasture, it attends too much to his reliance on technology. Technology is a vexed category in Berry's work, indispensable to the agrarian community he loves yet implicated in that community's economic and ecological decline. In "Damage" he enlists a notion of proportionate scale to set necessary technological limits: only tools that require no more than the faculties proper to a human body are permitted. He cites William Blake: "No bird soars too high, if he soars with his own wings." The solution is attractive in its appeal to the body as the most basic given of human experience, witness to our particularity and our creaturely dependence. But it falls apart under the weight of the poem's moral logic. If Berry had used man-powered shovels to dig the pond with his neighbors instead of a bulldozer, would the damaged earth still have fallen? Yes, probably. Shovels themselves multiply the power proper to the human body with leverage; furthermore, they require extrahuman power in their fabrication.

Berry needs a more coherent treatment of the problem of technology, its origin and its limits. Our Genesis text suggests a possibility, in its characteristically elliptical way. This second creation narrative, in contrast to the first, portrays creation as a manual labor of making and manipulating materials, a meaning that Alter captures in the term *fashion*:

> The Lord God fashioned the human, humus from the soil, and blew into his nostrils the breath of life.... And the Lord God fashioned from the wild each beast of the field and each fowl.... And the Lord God built the rib that he had taken from the human into a woman. (Genesis 2:7, 19, 22)

Yahweh is a craftsman, an artisan, but curiously the text mentions no tools. He uses existing materials but only the faculties of his own personage. This maker takes Berry's principle of *sola soma* to its fulfillment: all techne, no technology. Tools appear in Eden first in the hands of the humans, immediately following their meal of forbidden fruit: "And the eyes of the two were opened, and they knew they were naked, and they sewed fig leaves and made themselves loincloths" (Genesis 3:7). This passage is commonly understood to comment on shame or a civilizing process, but at least as interesting here is the appearance of technology, the needle and the cutting tool implied in the act of sewing. What interests me here is the sequence: desiring, consuming, knowing, and making. The humans figuratively remake the given world in a fantasy of availability, they consume the desired object, they know, and with their new knowledge they physically remake a world suddenly replete with tools and inert material. The anxiety and dislocation the humans experience after they eat the fruit, the self-deception and blame-dodging, the alienation that distorts their relationships to the soil and its creatures: all these may be read as bitter sequel to humanity's technological turn. They turn away from the given world and toward a world of their own making.

Relevant to this sequential instrumentalization is the work of theologian David Schindler, which develops a concept of a "technological ontology." Schindler's work focuses on post-Enlightenment modernity, but the process he describes is prefigured in Genesis. For Schindler, technology does not primarily consist in the made objects themselves; indeed, "it is the essence of the technological worldview that it perceives technology more or less simply as the sum of the things that are made . . . and that it then begins to assess these only in terms of how they are used."[12] This, to return now to Berry, is the first error in "Damage," recognizing as technology only the bulldozer instead of his own instrumental worldview, an ontology that is merely realized by the machine.

Properly understood, "a technological logic, or ordering intelligence," Schindler continues, "can be said to consist in . . . the conflation of knowing and making." Schindler relies here on the work of George Grant, the mid-century Canadian philosopher. Grant shows that "the modern West has ever-more pervasively conflated knowing—that is, conflated the human being's original presence to and in the world—with making. Missing from this presence-as-making, we may anticipate with our own terms, is an anterior sense of presence-as-being-given: of

---

12. Schindler, *Ordering Love*, 279.

being, ours and the world's, as gift."[13] Schindler continues: the "technological approach to knowledge has transformed that world into … something that is always yet to acquire its worth through its being-used or being-available-for-manipulation."[14]

Here, then, is the biblical text's gift to Berry: recognition that the instrumentalizing drive to make, not the nature of the tool, is the beginning of technology's corruption of creaturely relationships. Adam stitches leaves into loincloths, surely a harmless exploitation in itself. But the process inaugurates a human mode of encounter with the world as available, usable, and manipulable: the world as empty space rather than morally meaningful place. So totalizing is this technological ontology that Berry fails to recognize it in himself, blinded by the bulldozer. It is Berry's own appetite for pasture and his will to make what is not given that cause the earth to fall.

Such is the hard lesson of Genesis for Wendell Berry. Now it is Berry's turn to teach: what wisdom does "Damage" offer the Genesis narrative? The question circles around the tree of knowledge. The tree is cynosure and cypher at the center of the text: irresistibly present, intractably resistant to interpretation. No doubt I tread dangerously in hazarding a reading of my own.

We find the beginning of Berry's wisdom in a persistent theme running through his work: the limit to human understanding, a limit he experiences as a grace. Fritz Oehlschlaeger summarizes Berry's view thus: "If we … see mystery only as a kind of intolerable limit to our certainties, to our mastery of the world, then we will never be led into the slow revealing of what is to come, now and beyond. The foreclosure of mystery in favor of universal certainty—particularly as evidenced by E. O. Wilson in *Consilience*—is what Berry takes aim at."[15] Berry was an early articulator of the epistemology that has rooted deeply in the localist movement: the view that knowledge is local, not general; limited, not expansive; placed, not unified; contingent, not objective. His critique of overweening "consilient"—that is, totalizing, quantifiable—knowledge

---

13. Quoted in Schindler, *Ordering Love*, 277–78.
14. Schindler, *Ordering Love*, 278.
15. Oehlschlaeger, *Achievement of Wendell Berry*, 82.

has transmogrified in some quarters of localism into an unfortunate and, in my view, unwarranted suspicion of science.

A more interesting direction to take this strand of Berry's thought is mapped in "Damage." The poem introduces another term into his epistemology: *subject.* This is gentle wordplay. He uses the word at line level to mean the great subject or topic of his lifetime of writing, namely, the agrarian landscapes and communities of his native Kentucky—his thick place. Where he once thought of his writing as an escape from the world,

> I am no longer able to think that way. That is because I now live in my subject. My subject is my place in the world, and I live in my place.

> There is a sense in which I no longer "go to work." If I live in my place, which is my subject, then I am "at" my work even when I am not working.

But as the passage continues, the subject of his writing opens into a wider notion of subject as self:

> If I live in my subject, then writing about it cannot "free" me of it or "get it out of my system." When I am finished writing, I can only return to what I have been writing about.

Indeed, we are never free of subjectivity: our biases and blindness, our appetite and ego circumscribe the horizons of our knowledge. Our knowledge is local because our subject is placed. This suggests the modesty proper to human knowledge. If our subject is placed, our fantasies of autonomy and omnipotence are gutted: we find ourselves enmeshed in and thus vulnerable to the totality of the given world. A sparrow falls; an earthwork falls; two naked farmers in a garden fall. As Berry puts it:

If I have damaged my subject, then I have damaged my art. What aspired to be whole has met damage face to face, and has come away wounded.

For Berry, this insight is sobering but not devastating. He continues:

It accepts the clarification of pain, and concerns itself with healing. It cultivates the scar that is the course of time and nature over damage: the landmark and mindmark that is the notation of a limit.

To lose the scar of knowledge is to renew the wound.

An art that heals and protects its subject is a geography of scars.

Here, then, is Berry's gift to Adam and Eve: a damaged map of a scarred land. When they leave the garden, they enter a "geography of scars"; Adam must work to "cultivate [this] scar that is the course of time and nature over damage." When they leave the garden, Adam and Eve, like Berry, will live in their subject, and thus live thickly in their place: subject to local meanings and local limits, subject to the givenness of place. When Adam sweats, he will seek shade under the tree of scarred knowledge, "the landmark and mindmark that is the notation of a limit."

Where, then, do these narratives lead us? Each text fills an emptiness at the center of the other: we learn from Genesis that the tool-in-mind, an instrumentalizing appetite to transform the world for our use, precedes the tool-in-hand; we learn from Berry that the tree of knowledge marks the limitation of human understanding. Taken together, does this fullness merely lead to a counsel of despair? Is there escape from the collusion of human appetite and technological ontology that locks us into an instrumentalizing relationship with the world? Are we consigned by our natures to ever re-create our environment in the projected image of our own fantasies, and thus to live always in a closed system of exploitation and disappointment?

The texts themselves do not answer these questions. Instead, I offer in conclusion two passages that gesture toward a route forward. Schindler writes:

> It is crucial to understand, however, that the instrumental character of things follows ontologically from what is always already their inherently given truth and goodness and beauty, *because it is the nature of the good to share itself.* The instrumentality of nature, in other words, can never be taken legitimately to mean that things in their natural givenness are merely "brute facts," awaiting the simply utilitarian meaning that is to be assigned them, now arbitrarily, by human beings. The necessary and legitimate instrumentality of nature, in a word, must be seen from within, and as a sign and expression of, what is the intrinsic or transcendental truth and goodness and beauty of things qua created and thus given: as a sign and expression, indeed, of things' basic liturgical and covenantal meaning in relation to God.[16]

It is the nature of the good to share itself. The inherent goodness of creation, a notion carried over from the first cosmogony of Genesis, means that natural world not only has intrinsic value and purpose, but *offers that essence to the human mind in a gesture of covenant relationality.* The creatureliness of the world itself, bearing as it does the imprint of the Creator in its very sovereignty, invites us to partake. Emmanuel Levinas gets at something similar when he writes:

> We live from "good soup," air, light, spectacles, work, ideas, sleep, etc. . . . These are not objects of representations. *We live from them.* Nor is what we live from a "means of life," as the pen is a means with respect to the letter it permits us to write—nor a goal of life, as communication is the goal of the letter. The things we live from

---

16. Schindler, *Ordering Love*, 9.

are not tools, nor even implements, in the Heideggerian sense of the term. Their existence is not exhausted by the utilitarian schematism that delineates them as having the existence of hammers, needles, or machines. They are always in a certain measure—and even the hammers, needles, and machines are—objects of enjoyment, presenting themselves to "taste," already adorned, embellished. Moreover, whereas the recourse to the instrument implies finality and indicates a dependence with regard to the other, living from ... delineates independence itself, the independence of enjoyment and of its happiness, which is the original pattern of all independence.[17]

Consistent with Schindler's suggestion, Levinas finds that the world—including the human-built entities in that world—"presents itself" to human perception as a gift of inherent beauty and happiness, independent from its utilitarian function. To this Levinas adds an insightful distinction between "living off of" and "living from" our place. To *live off of* the earth is to exhaust the meaning of its existence in service of our own ends. To *live from* the "good soup" or good soil of the world, in contrast, is to recognize the delight-in-existence of the hundreds of entities sharing the world with us at every moment in time: even the papers, the telephone, the scissors, and the keyboard that offer themselves to my perception at this moment are pregnant with goodness and tendering partnership with my hands.

Here perhaps is hope for the humans in Eden. Yes, the technological ontology, the tool-in-mind, always threatens to reduce human knowing to making and acting upon, to resolve all flesh into the old question "Who, whom?" Human knowing is itself inescapably partial, biased, scarred, positioned. Yet this need not consign us, like a Sisyphean blacksmith, to an eternity of frantically fabricating the bars that imprison our own minds. The fruit that the humans eat and the leaves they stitch, if Schindler and Levinas are right, present themselves,

---

17. Emmanuel Levinas, *Totality and Infinity: An Essay on Exteriority*, trans. Alphonso Lingis (Pittsburgh: Duquense University Press, 1969), 110.

with their inherent qualities and purposes, as potential partners to the humans in the cosmic dance of time. If the humans lay *consecrated* hands on the fruit, or the shovel, or, yes, even the bulldozer, hands that know their own creatureliness and honor the creatureliness of the world they encounter, then the gesture is not instrumental but covenantal. The earth and all its good soil fall not downward but outward, toward place, encounter, and relationship.

Theoscatology: On Dirt, Dung, and Digestion in God's Garden

Adam S. Miller

Thy mind, O man! if thou wilt lead a soul unto salvation, must stretch as high as the utmost heavens, and search into and contemplate the darkest abyss, and the broad expanse of eternity—thou must commune with God.
—Joseph Smith, *History of the Church*, 3:295

That which is spiritual being in the likeness of that which is temporal; and that which is temporal in the likeness of that which is spiritual; the spirit of man in the likeness of his person, as also the spirit of every beast, and every other creature which God has created.
—Doctrine and Covenants 77:2

1. The kind of thing a body is

MORMONS BELIEVE THAT WE NEED BODIES to become like God. But bodies are organs of passing. Bodies channel what they can of the world through narrow walls of flesh and bone. Bodies pass light through our eyes, sounds through our ears, smells through our noses, tastes through our tongues, food through our bowels, air through our lungs, blood through our veins, electricity through our nerves, and symbols through our brains. These things all come and these things all go.

But, especially, bodies are built around our need for food. We have brains, but these brains sit on top of a mouth on top of a stomach on top of some eight meters of bowels. We have hearts for circulating food, lungs for burning food, nervous systems for detecting food, brains for plotting about food, and limbs for chasing it down. We put the world in our mouths and the world passes through us. Our bodies borrow their living from the world. For both the eater and the eaten, this borrowing is costly. And no matter how much our brains or lungs or bowels manage to sponge, there's always a remainder. You can keep part of what you take in, but only for a time. No matter how stuffed we feel, our bowels will move again. No matter how full our lungs, we will exhale. No matter how clear the thought, we will think the next thing.

We could draft a whole taxonomy of possible theologies just in terms of how they deal with these passings and their remainders. A short survey would suffice:

What is your theology's position on digestion?

a. Excrement is a regrettable, local, temporary phenomenon.
b. Excrement is so essential to bodies that such remainders are eternal.

In many ways, this indelicate question is *the* theological question. How we choose to answer will decide how we treat time and how we think about matter. It will shape our understanding of creation, agency, desire, sin, and redemption.

If bodies are organs of passing, will resurrection bring all of this passing—all of this waxing and waning, this wanting and detesting, this flooding and emptying, this inhaling and exhaling, this endless digesting—to an end? Do resurrected lungs exhale? Do perfected bowels move? Is the remainder real? Is it divine?

Living bodies are porous. Would a resurrected body cease to be porous? And if it did, would it still be a body? Living bodies are membranes, filters for sifting the world. Would a resurrected body cease to be a membrane? And if it did, would it still be human? Living bodies are planted in ecological interdependence. Do resurrected bodies belong to their worlds? Does life circulate in heaven? Is it shared? Would a resurrected body cease to be ecological? And if it did, would it still count as alive?

If we reread the biblical account of the Garden of Eden with these questions in mind, what might we see with new eyes?

2. A methodological note

In what follows I will offer a reading of Genesis 2–3 (just one among many possible readings) that is not literal or metaphorical but instrumental. When, in Genesis 2–3, the story talks about trees, fruit, dirt, breath, and bodies, I will not treat these as symbols in need of decoding. I will just treat them as referring to trees, fruit, dirt, breath, and bodies. However, I will also not read this story literally, as if it referred simply to two particular people at one particular place and time. Rather, I will treat this garden story about dirt, fruit, and digestion instrumentally, as a constellation of ideas capable of leveraging our relationship to dirt and digestion into a different configuration. In other words, I will read this story as if it taught "nothing save it were repentance and faith on the Lord" (Mosiah 18:20).

3. Humans from the humus

It is commonplace in biblical commentaries to note the difference in tone between the first creation story in Genesis 1:1–2:4 and the second account that begins abruptly midway through Genesis 2:4.[1] Where the tone of the first creation story is high and formal, the second is colloquial and earthy. Where the first looks down on creation from a grand cosmic perspective, the second unfolds at ground level and on a human scale. Where the first tells how God created "heaven and

---

1. The transition from one account to the next in the middle of verse 4 is not clearly rendered in the King James translation of the passage. I will include below a clearer translation that is more faithful to the Hebrew.

earth" (Genesis 1:1), the second inverts the prior formula and, instead, tells how God created "earth and heaven" (Genesis 2:4). Where the grammar in the first account is paced, stately, and symmetrical, the grammar in the second, as Robert Alter notes, "begins with elaborate syntactical subordination in a long complex sentence that uncoils all the way from the second part of verse 4 to the end of verse 7." More, in this second account, God "does not summon things into being from a lofty distance through the mere agency of divine speech, but works as a craftsman ... blowing life-breath into nostrils, building a woman from a rib. Whatever the disparate historical origins of the two accounts, the redaction gives us first a harmonious cosmic overview of creation and then a plunge into the technological nitty-gritty and moral ambiguities of human origins."[2]

Alter's translation[3] of the grammatically complex overture to the second narrative reads like this:

On the day the LORD God made earth and heavens, no shrub of the field being yet on the earth and no plant of the field yet sprouted, for the LORD God had not caused rain to fall on the earth and there was no human to till the soil, and wetness would well from the earth to water all the surface of the soil, then the LORD God fashioned the human, humus from the soil, and blew into his nostrils the breath of life, and the human became a living creature. (Genesis 2:4–7)

The syntactical complexity of this opening section signals, like a warning shot across the reader's bow, a dramatic shift in tone and perspective. The grammar foreshadows the kind of thematic complexity and ambiguity characteristic of the very human story that follows. In a single opening line, the text introduces us—all at once and in a jumble—to a host of actors, conditions, and locations: God, earth,

---

2. Robert Alter, *The Five Books of Moses: A Translation with Commentary* (New York: W. W. Norton, 2004), 20.

3. Unless otherwise noted, I will use Alter's translations of Genesis throughout as found in his *Five Books of Moses*.

heaven, shrubs, fields, rain, soil, dampness, tilling, the human, nostrils, breath, blowing, fashioning, and so on. The rush to squeeze all of these elements into a single opening line, as if no one of them could be introduced without at least mentioning the others that condition and situate them, hints at the ecological complexity of the creative act itself. As many elements as the text can manage must be laid out immediately and in tight proximity. Further, the passage's complex temporal braid of present, projected, and consequent actions is especially striking as it toggles back and forth between what has happened, what hasn't yet happened, and what will need to happen for the pieces of the world to be bootstrapped into a workable ecology. The temporality proper to this second account of creation is not linear. Rather, time gets structured by the same press of complex, interdependent feedback loops that, shortly, will also structure the initial human experience—especially for Eve— of good, evil, and desire.

Note, too, that this second account of creation quickly zeroes in on a key word that is entirely absent from the first creation account. While both the first and second stories talk about God's creation of "the earth" (*ha'arets*), the second story immediately focuses its attention on "the soil" (*'adamah*). This shift from the earth (in general) to the soil (in particular) is pivotal for the arc of the second story because, in this version, God is going to fashion the human itself (*'adam*) out of the soil (*'adamah*). To be a human being, the story indicates, is to be soil that breathes. "Then the Lord God fashioned the human, humus from the soil, and blew into his nostrils the breath of life, and the human became a living creature" (Genesis 2:7). This is no metaphor. Ashes to ashes, dust to dust: humans depend on the soil, our bodies are made from soil, and those bodies will literally become soil once again. To be a human being is to be a shaped membrane of local elements put into a relation of active, ecological interdependence with its local environment. This ecological interdependence initially takes the form of respiration: the circulation of oxygen and carbon dioxide immediately embeds the human in a web of borrowed and co-conditioned strengths.

Soil itself recapitulates the temporally complex feedback loops crucial to sustaining life because soil, though it must in some sense precede plant and animal life, is itself alive and, more, is itself composed, in part, of decomposing plants and animals. Plants can't grow without soil, but soil is itself composed of dead plants. Animals can't eat fruit that trees haven't grown, but trees need the seeded dung that follows from eating fruit to root new trees. The world is a confusion of overlapping membranes that sift each other's remainders. Life, as ecological, consists of feedback loops embedded inside feedback loops. Ecosystems depend on the generation of these mutually anterior dependences.

After God breathes into the shaped soil and the human comes to life, God places the human in the garden "to till it and to watch it." Then God "commanded the human, saying, 'From every fruit of the garden you may surely eat. But from the tree of knowledge, good and evil, you shall not eat, for on the day you eat from it, you are doomed to die'" (Genesis 2:16–17). With some provisos about what's appropriate for food, God now directs the human not only to breathe but to eat. Further, God sees that, even well fed, it's "not good for the human to be alone," and after comically auditioning all the beasts of the field and fowls of the air for a companion, "the Lord God built the rib He had taken from the human into a woman" (Genesis 2:18, 22). The woman is now bone of the human's bone, flesh of his flesh, soil taken from his own breathing soil.

4. Eating the fruit

The story kicks into high gear, however, once the serpent arrives and tempts Eve to eat fruit from the tree of knowledge. If she eats it, the serpent says, "you shall not be doomed to die. For God knows that on the day you eat of it your eyes will be opened and you will become as gods knowing good and evil" (Genesis 3:4–5). The woman here is promised a very particular kind of knowledge. If she eats this fruit, she will be introduced, in the first person, to the costs of life, both good and evil.

Now, again, I don't intend to read the fruit in this story metaphorically or supernaturally. Rather, I want to read the fruit as fruit, and in particular, I want to read the eating of it as, in fact, an *eating*. "And the woman saw that the tree was good for eating and that it was lust to the eyes and the tree was lovely to look at, and she took of its fruit and ate, and she also gave to her man, and he ate. And the eyes of the two were opened, and they knew they were naked, and they sewed fig leaves and made themselves loincloths" (Genesis 3:6–7).

Note that the woman only eats the fruit (fruit that she must first, presumably, eat in order to know what is and isn't good) because she *already* sees that "the tree is good." As with the soil, her action presupposes a knowledge that the action itself is meant to account for. And note, too, that the immediate result is that after eating this fruit, both of the humans begin to feel shame (cf. Genesis 2:25) and rush to cover their nakedness. Suddenly, the humans are in need of fig leaves.

It is common to think that, because the humans are naked, their embarrassment has something to do with sex. But it's not clear to me what sex has to do with the kind of knowledge one acquires by eating fruit. For my part, I don't think that this pivotal revelation about the nature of good and evil was initially about sex. I think it was about digestion. This reading may involve less high-romantic drama and more low comedy, but what other kind of revelation would inevitably follow when you've eaten too much fruit? The humans may have rushed to cover their nakedness, but they weren't covering their sex. They were covering their sphincters. Shocked and ashamed and afraid, the humans were suddenly brought face to face with what it would *cost* to be a living, breathing thing: the consumption of other living things. And, more, they were brought face to face with the truth of what it means to be dirt that, digesting its world, will always leave a remainder that must itself be expelled as dirt.

Eating this fruit, the humans discover how death is intertwined with life. They discover how their bodies, shaped from dirt, were *built for* consumption and defecation.

Whether the humans had been ingesting and digesting and egesting all along in the garden, the story doesn't say. God permits them to eat the other fruits. But if they had been eating, it seems they didn't yet know what it meant. They didn't yet know what it meant to be a membrane. And once they found out, they wished they hadn't. Finding themselves embodied, they flinched at the cost.

The scriptures are full of talk about bowels, both human and divine. But, as John Durham Peters puts it in a beautiful article, "Bowels of Mercy," published in *BYU Studies*,

the bowels are subjects about which we are often embar-
rassed to talk. And yet the scriptures put the bowels
unavoidably in our face. Our resistance to reflection about
bowels is itself instructive. The bowels sit at the center of
the human body and yet nothing is so furtive as the act
of doing our business. But it is an experience "common
to man," one to which we can all relate and one we all
had to master at an early age. The bowels may repulse
us, but few distresses are as acute as when they malfunc-
tion. Bowels are the part of embodied life which we rarely
articulate but which is most intimately our own. When
they are discussed, they are usually the stuff of bawdy
humor, snickering puerility, or scatological writing, not
scriptural truth. The bowels may be the most personal and
hidden of all organs. The sheer relief of the bowels being
moved—the release of inner containment—may serve as a
secret metaphor of what it is to go beyond ourselves, to let
our insides go, to stop holding back. Perhaps in some ways,
compassion, as the Greek suggests, has a similar motion.[4]

In the aftermath of digestion, one can imagine our primal parents
suffering the kind of terrifying, telescoping vision suffered by tennis
prodigy Hal Incandenza in David Foster Wallace's novel *Infinite Jest*.
Late in the novel, Hal, a teenage tennis prodigy, has a vision where the
collective, horrifying weight of a lifetime's worth of food is exhibited
to him in a single stroke. Hal says:

The familiarity of Academy routine took on a crushing
cumulative aspect. . . . I re-experienced the year's total
number of steps, movements, the breaths and pulses
involved. Then the number of times I would have to
repeat the same processes, day after day, in all kinds of
light, until I graduated and moved away and then began
the same exhausting processes of exit and return in some

---

4. John Durham Peters, "Bowels of Mercy," *BYU Studies* 38/4 (1999): 32.

dormitory at some tennis-power university somewhere. Maybe the worst part of the cognitions involved the incredible volume of food I was going to have to consume over the rest of my life. Meal after meal, plus snacks. Day after day after day. Experiencing this food in toto. Just the thought of the meat alone. One megagram? Two megagrams? I experienced, vividly, the image of a broad cool well-lit room piled floor to ceiling with nothing but the lightly breaded chicken fillets I was going to consume over the next sixty years. The number of fowl vivisected for a lifetime's meat. The amount of hydrochloric acid and bilirubin and glucose and glycogen and gloconol produced and absorbed and produced in my body. And another, dimmer room, filled with the rising mass of the excrement I'd produce, the room's double-locked steel door gradually bowing outward with the mounting pressure.... I had to put my hand out against the wall and stand there hunched until the worst of [this vision] passed.[5]

With the revelation of good and evil vouchsafed, the humans now find themselves in a similar position. Having eaten the fruit, they now *knew the truth about hunger*: though they'd chewed the fruit up (and it was delicious), the fruit wasn't enough, and what the fruit did give, they couldn't keep. They saw what the gods see. Hunger is real. Death is the price of life. And they, too—ashes to ashes, dirt to dirt—were going to die.

This is a hard thing to see. The humans wanted to run away. They wanted to hide. They didn't want to face the passing that, in their flesh, they themselves gave body to. They didn't want to deal with the dirt that composed them or the dirt they expelled from themselves. They wished with all their might for that not-yet-invented-but-originally-sinful thing: a really powerful toilet. They wished for something to flush the truth away.

This Edenic fantasy of flight and flushing finds its apotheosis in Wallace's quasi-journalistic essay "A Supposedly Fun Thing I'll Never

---

5. David Foster Wallace, *Infinite Jest* (New York: Back Bay Books, 2006), 897.

Do Again." For seven days and six nights, Wallace carefully traces how all the tiny details of his luxury Caribbean cruise collude to promote the fantasy of a gratification that will (finally!) neither pass nor disappoint, producing a satisfaction without remainder. The sales pitch is simple: on this luxury cruise, with its eleven-plus gourmet meals per day, all of your needs will be met. The meals, the massages, the entertainment, the weather, the pampering, the comfort, the company—all of it—will be, for once, *enough*. This fantasy comes to a head in Wallace's description of cabin 1009's astonishing toilet:

> But all this is still small potatoes compared to 1009's fascinating and potentially malevolent toilet. A harmonious concordance of elegant form and vigorous function, flanked by rolls of tissue so soft as to be without the usual perforates for tearing, my toilet has above it this sign:
>
> THIS TOILET IS CONNECTED TO A VACUUM SEWAGE SYSTEM. PLEASE DO NOT THROW INTO THE TOILET ANYTHING THAN ORDINARY TOILET WASTE AND TOILET PAPER [*sic*]
>
> Yes that's right a *vacuum toilet*. And, as with the exhaust fan above, not a lightweight or unambitious vacuum. The toilet's flush produces a brief but traumatizing sound, a kind of held high-B gargle, as of some gastric disturbance on a cosmic scale. Along with this sound comes a concussive suction so awesomely powerful that it's both scary and strangely comforting—your waste seems less removed than *hurled* from you, and hurled with a velocity that lets you feel as though the waste is going to end up someplace so far away from you that it will have become an abstraction . . . a kind of existential-level sewage treatment.[6]

---

6. David Foster Wallace, *A Supposedly Fun Thing I'll Never Do Again: Essays and Arguments* (New York: Back Bay Books, 1998), 304–5, emphasis in original.

In one sense, this is the fundamental human fantasy. The fantasy we buy (again and again) is of an "existential-level sewage treatment" that will free us from life's troubles and costs, a treatment whose awesomely powerful suction will comfort us with the sheer concussive force of its vacuum-powered denial: There is no passing here! You are not dirt expelling dirt!

The serpent sells the humans this same old story: you can eat without death or defecation, you can enjoy without cost or loss, you can fill your stomach and stay full, you can live without dying. Commenting on the implicit promise of his luxury cruise, Wallace sums up this idolatrous fantasy:

> We're maybe now in a position to appreciate the lie at the dark heart of Celebrity's brochure. For this—the promise to sate the part of me that always and only WANTS—is the central fantasy the brochure is selling. The thing to notice is that the real fantasy here isn't that this promise will be kept, but that such a promise is keepable at all. This is a big one, this lie. And of course I want to believe it ... I want to believe that maybe this Ultimate Fantasy Vacation will be *enough* pampering, that this time the luxury and pleasure will be so completely and faultlessly administered that my Infantile part will be sated. But the Infantile part of me is insatiable.[7]

Theologically, we might critique this kind of high-tech porcelain idolatry in one of two ways. (And the difference between these two possible responses hinges on how we answer the survey question with which this essay began.)

1. On the one hand, we might say that the luxury cruise's "existential-level sewage treatment" is an idol, a false god,

---

7. Wallace, *Supposedly Fun Thing*, 316–17, emphasis in original.

because only God can actually deliver on the promise of a satisfaction without passing and without remainder.

2. Or, on the other hand, we might say that cabin 1009's industrial-strength toilet is an idol, a false god, because God *intends* us to have (and keep) bodies that fundamentally are and will eternally remain *organs of passing*.

Again, this is not an idle theological question. What we think life is, what we think our bodies are, what we think sin is, and what we think redemption looks like will depend on whether we think the fantasy is sound (though perhaps only possible in a perfected heaven where life has no costs, bodies are not membranes, and living is not ecological) or whether we think this fantasy itself smells of fear, shame, and sin. In one story, the humans became sinners because they got dirty. In the other story, they became sinners because they didn't want to be dirt.

We might pose the question like this: does Christ's resurrection conquer *death*, or does it conquer *dying*? At present, life passes in us *as* a kind of dying. Does Christ save us from life as a passing and dying? Or does Christ save us from death as what brings this business of passing and dying (that is, life) to an end? We might also frame the issue a bit more abstractly. Metaphysically, the issue at stake is twofold. Is it possible to exist without cost and loss? And is it possible to relate without remainder?

5. The divinely appointed human task

In closing, I want to note how the story in God's garden ends. The story, we've seen, begins with God planting a garden and gathering that garden's rich and fragrant humus into the shape of a human. Then, with a kiss, God breathes life into that soil. After the humans have eaten the fruit of the tree of knowledge and hidden their bodies—from each other and from God—God sorts the mess by commanding Adam to spend the rest of his life trying to grow a garden of his own.

> And to the human He said, "Because you listened to the voice of your wife and ate from the tree that I commanded you, 'You shall not eat from it,'

> Cursed shall be the soil for your sake,
> with pangs shall you eat from it all the days of your life.
> Thorn and thistle shall it sprout for you
> and you shall eat the plants of the field.
> By the sweat of your brow shall you eat bread
> till you return to the soil,
> for from there were you taken,
> for dust you are
> and to dust shall you return." (Genesis 3:17–19)

God imposes on the human a very specific task, and he does so for, what seems to me, a very specific reason: the human needs to be taught a lesson, and to learn it he'll have to spend his life tilling the soil. He'll have to pass his days up to his elbows in dirt, and when he sits down to eat his sweaty bread, he'll find the smell of soil clinging to his hands.

Why this job? The text is explicit. The human's job is to spend his life working with the soil because he *is* soil. "By the sweat of your brow shall you eat bread till you return to the soil, for from there were you taken, for dirt you are and to dirt shall you return" (cf. Genesis 3:19). As John Durham Peters notes in this same vein: "More than any other organ, however, the bowels most ally us to the soil. We have, one might say, a long compost pit within. Our bowels add to the earth and remind us daily that we inhabit tabernacles of clay."[8] We are, in truth, walking colonies of compost. We are brightly burning engines of decomposition.

We might read this "curse" as penal, but I think that would be a mistake. I think the human's assignment is primarily pedagogical. The human needs to understand what kind of thing a body is and what kind of complex and costly entanglements that body depends on. The human recoiled from his own waste, but now, by divine design, his job is to spend his life coming to appreciate just what that magic ingredient is that will make a beautiful living garden grow. Through the human's digging and planting and dunging (as the Lord and his servants all do in God's vineyard), the nature of an embodied life will become clear to

---

8. Peters, "Bowels of Mercy," 32.

him. Day by day, meal by meal, squat by squat, the human will cultivate his garden and meditate on its passing. Gradually, a stillness will settle in him that results not from the absence but from the presence of life's passing. Relieved, he'll expel a long, deep breath. And, more, he'll come to feel that he shares with all of the world's saints and sinners, down through all of time's passing, that same theoscatological imperative:

> Something humble, placid even, about inert feet under stall doors. The defecatory posture is an accepting posture, it occurs to him. Head down, elbows on knees, the fingers laced together between the knees. Some hunched timeless millennial type of waiting, almost religious. Luther's shoes on the floor beneath the chamber pot, placid, possibly made of wood, Luther's 16th-century shoes, awaiting epiphany. The mute quiescent suffering of generations of salesmen in the stalls of train-station johns, heads down, fingers laced, shined shoes inert, awaiting the acid gush. Women's slippers, centurion's dusty sandals, dock-workers' hobnailed boots, Pope's slippers. All waiting, pointing straight ahead, slightly tapping. Huge shaggy-browed men in skins hunched just past the firelight's circle with wadded leaves in one hand, waiting.[9]

Partaking of the fruit of the tree of knowledge, the human will open his eyes. And then, by God's grace, he'll become like the gods themselves and his bowels will be filled with mercy.

---

9. Wallace, *Infinite Jest*, 103.

"And It Came to Pass": A Response to Adam Miller's "Theoscatology"

Joseph M. Spencer

DESCRIBING WHAT HE CALLED the "prosy detail of imaginary history" he found in the Book of Mormon, Mark Twain said the following of the formula that marks the narrative movement of the book: "'And it came to pass' was [the translator's] pet. If he had left that out, his Bible would have been only a pamphlet."[1] Twain is, of course, hardly the only reader to have noted—and to have complained about—the ceaseless repetition of this formula in the text of the Book of Mormon. Some French editions, for instance, have replaced the formula with an asterisk, not quite making a pamphlet of the book, but shortening it substantially nonetheless.[2] "Scores" of the iterated formula were removed by the Community of Christ committee tasked with producing a reader-friendly Revised Authorized Version of the Book of Mormon.[3] And Joseph Smith himself removed a number of instances of

---

1. Mark Twain, *Roughing It* (New York: Signet, 1980), 103.

2. See Grant Hardy, *Understanding the Book of Mormon: A Reader's Guide* (New York: Oxford University Press, 2010), 5.

3. See Richard P. Howard, *Restoration Scriptures: A Study of Their Textual Development* (Independence, MO: Reorganized Church of Jesus Christ of Latter Day Saints, 1969), 62.

the formula from the book for the second edition in 1837, presumably in part because he had already begun to hear complaints (if not to make them himself!) regarding the frequency of the formula's appearance.[4]

Frankly, readers of the Book of Mormon very quickly get tired of the phrase—"and it came to pass," "and it came to pass," "and it came to pass." When we set out from Jerusalem with Nephi at the book's beginning, we feel its pinch. By the time we've crossed a desert and an ocean and arrived in the New World, we can tell that it's giving us blisters. When we later find ourselves trudging back and forth between the lands of Nephi and Zarahemla, or marching on the campaign trail with Captain Moroni, or standing precariously atop the wall with Samuel the Lamanite, the phrase has long since rubbed our flesh raw. Much as we might hope for healing from the visiting Christ of 3 Nephi, we never find release. Right through to the end of the Book of Mormon, we're reading the refrain: "and it came to pass," "and it came to pass," "and it came to pass."

But I find myself wondering, after reading Adam Miller's reflections on "theoscatology," whether the often-mentioned Mormon appreciation for the body shouldn't make us pause reflectively at every "and it came to pass." "We need bodies to become like God," Miller says, "but bodies are organs of passing." What's packed into the Book of Mormon's repetitive formula, this textual and narrative remainder that we'd prefer to elide or at least to replace with a contentless asterisk? What might we find if we were to read "and it came to pass" as a *theological* formula?

The construction of the formula is important, I think. The only parallel construction to "it came to pass" of which I can think is "it came to be." Note the difference, however. In "it came to be," we have a certain formulaic dismantling of becoming, a certain cancellation of the dynamic and the mobile. The formula opens ("it came ...") with change and modulation, in fact with *becoming*, but it closes ("... to be") with an interruption of change and modulation, in fact with *being*. "It came to be": static being, as a kind of telos, brings becoming to an end.

---

4. See Royal Skousen, *Analysis of Textual Variants of the Book of Mormon, Part 1: Title Page, Witness Statements, 1 Nephi 1–2 Nephi 10* (Provo, UT: FARMS, 2004), 207.

All transformation culminates in a certain *state*, a final *form*. It *came*, yes—but it came only in order to *be*.[5]

What, though, of "it came to pass"? Here the dynamic is succeeded not by the static but by the dynamic. Change and transformation culminate in change and transformation. It came—not *to be* but *to pass*. Might we say, "it came *in order* to pass"? Its purpose or its telos, if *it* can be said to have one, *is* to pass, to remain in the flux of becoming. There's no shift from becoming to being, no end of history. There's only coming and going, the approach of the open from the future and the passage of the closed into the past. There's only, in other words, the persistent punctuation of what, in an earlier version of "Theoscatology," Miller called "intra-thoracic time."

But that's too simple, isn't it? What of the tension between the infinitive *to pass* and the conjugated *it came*? Might there be a kind of shift as becoming gives way to passing—a shift, though, not from becoming to being but from the actual to the potential? The formula speaks not of what is *coming* but of what *came*. The first part of the formula—"it came"—already freezes becoming, calcifies the impersonal *it*, stops the heart whose pulse marks the rhythm of time. In "it came" we have the full realization of the actual. But then the frozen, the calcified, the stopped, the fully realized, the actual—*this* passes from actuality to potentiality, from finitude (the closedness of what *has passed*: "it came") to the infinite (the neither-past-nor-present-*nor-future* status of what remains *infinitive*: "to pass"). In "it came to pass," perhaps we witness the determinate become indeterminate, the decided become undecidable. In pass*ing*, what *came* (what, indeed, came *to be*) reclaims potentiality (and therefore power?) by a Bartlebian "preferring not to,"[6] by passing over its being and retrieving the becoming it would seem to have given up in the *past* tense of "it came," transforming "the past" (or "the passed") into "to pass."

---

5. We find something much the same in constructions that replace the impersonal *it* with the personal pronoun: "I came to realize" or "I came to see."

6. See Giorgio Agamben, "Bartleby, or On Contingency," in *Potentialities: Collected Essays in Philosophy*, ed. and trans. Daniel Heller-Roazen (Stanford: Stanford University Press, 1999), 243–71.

What is it "to pass," then? A first question. And a question, I fear, that's made relatively little sense as I've tried to develop it here. But let me complicate it further, nonetheless. What of the impersonal *it*? If it's difficult enough even to know what it means to speak, infinitively, of passing ("What is it 'to pass'?"), it's more difficult still to guess at what it means for *it* to pass, or for *it* to have come. What lies behind the *it* of "it came to pass"—or of "it came to be," for that matter? Why is *it* singular? Why is *it* neuter? Why is *it* indeterminate? More baffling, perhaps: Why is *it* there *at all*? Why not speak rather of what exactly it is that comes, that passes, that is? Why is it only *it* that "comes to pass"?

There's likely little to be decided immediately about *it*, so let me also leave it to one side in order to complicate things further in a second way—in a way that might be less confusing. Notice that I have simplified the Book of Mormon's formulation in much of this brief discussion—giving attention not to "*and* it came to pass" but simply to "it came to pass." What of the *and* that, far more often than not, introduces "it came to pass"? What of the conjunctive or connective function of the formula, its concatenating function? This is perhaps particularly important, since it's the *and* of "and it came to pass" that largely prescribes the frequency of its repetition in Book of Mormon narrative. (Indeed, we might well wonder whether it's the "it came to pass" or merely the *and* that drives us mad as readers of the Book of Mormon.)

Hiding behind the word *and* is a logical function, an operator that marks the status of statements whose connectedness serves as a condition of their collective truth. Things are a little more complicated than just that, since logical conjunction is actually a simplification of a more complex operation (to be specific: the negation of a positively conditioned negation).[7] For the moment, however, it suffices to say that *and* weaves into a kind of totality of causative and conditioning relations all of what language might correctly say about the world—the world

---

7. See Gottlob Frege, "*Begriffsschrift*, a Formula Language, Modeled upon That of Arithmetic, for Pure Thought," in *From Frege to Gödel: A Source Book in Mathematical Logic, 1879–1931*, ed. Jean van Heijenoort (Cambridge: Harvard University Press, 1967), 19.

of becoming as much as of the world of being.[8] What we have in "and it came to pass" is the continuing concatenation of statements about how history might be potentialized, might be given *to pass*.

It is thus in a double sense that we find in "and it came to pass" something like the *remainder* of the Book of Mormon. It's the book's remainder in that it's what we fantasize about flushing away, but it's also the book's remainder in that it's what marks the Book of Mormon's consistent attempt to repotentialize what might too easily become mere actuality. It's what, if we pay attention to its talk of passing, may alert us to how the book not only *reports* but also *questions* or even *contests* history. It's for that reason that, even and perhaps especially in reading the Book of Mormon, we need to shift our attention, as Miller says, from "high drama" to "low comedy," giving our attention to the excessive and overdetermined narrative the Book of Mormon weaves.

A final thought: Here, as elsewhere, I've tried to read Adam Miller as a Book of Mormon theologian—as a thinker of the tensions and stresses at work in the text that launched the history through which *we* are all passing, through which we'll *always* be passing.[9] Perhaps it's only wishful thinking on my part that finds me bringing Miller's thinking back to the Book of Mormon, a too-invested plea that he read less of Bruno Latour and David Foster Wallace and more of the brother of Jared and Alma the Elder. I think not, though. The more time I spend in conversation with Miller, the more I find the image Walter Benjamin took from Edgar Allen Poe to describe his own thought to be appropriate for making sense of Miller's work.[10] His readers and listeners experience him as an elaborately dressed Turk, playing a game

---

8. See Alfred Tarski, "The Concept of Truth in Formalized Languages," in *Logic, Semantics, Metamathematics*, 2nd ed., ed. John Corcoran, trans. J. H. Woodger (Indianapolis: Hackett, 1983), 187–88.

9. See Joseph M. Spencer, "Notes on Novelty," *SquareTwo* 6/1 (Spring 2013), http://squaretwo.org/Sq2ArticleMillerSymposiumSpencer.html.

10. See Walter Benjamin, "Theses on the Philosophy of History," in *Illuminations: Essays and Reflections*, ed. Hannah Arendt, trans. Harry Zohn (New York: Schocken Books, 2007), 253; and Giorgio Agamben, *The Time That Remains: A Commentary on the Letter to the Romans*, trans. Patricia Dailey (Stanford: Stanford University Press, 2005), 138–45.

of chess he always seems to be winning. But I've peeked under the table on which the chessboard sits, and I've seen that the Turk they see is only a massive puppet, entirely controlled by a little hunchback dwarf crouched beneath the table. It stays out of sight, for the most part, but it's what makes every successful move. And its name is the Book of Mormon.

Partaking of the Fruit of Ecological Wisdom: A Reading of Genesis 2–3 Applied to Environmental Education in Zion

Candice D. Wendt

Partaking of ecological wisdom: A soul-enlarging transformation

GENESIS 2–3 CAN BE INTERPRETED as a narrative about the process of human individuals gaining ecological awareness and commitment. In a crash course on botany, zoology, gardening, and other topics, Adam and Eve sit at the feet of the Creator of the earth; among other roles, the Lord serves as an environmental educator. In Eden, Eve and Adam begin to gain ecological competence, or the personal feelings of care and knowledge needed to sustain the natural systems that provide for life. Greater responsibility for creation comes as they seek and partake of wisdom, or the fruit of knowledge. The choice to taste the fruit bears special significance in an ecologically oriented reading; it can be understood as a demonstration of desire to become faithful and wise stewards of creation. Willingness matures into commitment as they make covenants with God and leave the garden to cultivate life outside it. As I reread Adam and Eve's experiences, I will argue that the pursuit of ecological wisdom is an important reason why the fall can be understood to be a soul-enlarging transformation for humanity.

Creator and creation as partakers of embodied knowledge

In Genesis 2–3 the Lord appears as an intimate, hands-on cultivator, partaker, and applier of knowledge in a physical world. He is a being with such rich understanding of anatomy and biological matter that he forms bodies with his hands like a potter and surgeon at once. He observes the opportune moment to create a living human soul, watching water flowing out of the ground onto the surface of the soil (Genesis 2:6). To him the dust covering the earth is a rich and valuable medium worth careful attention. He bends down and labors in it, gathering and generating form, color, function, and minute details. The Lord relates to earth as a caring, focused worker. He appears as someone who desires and needs to not only apply knowledge about how living souls work, but also create beings who can, like him, relate meaningfully in a physical world.

The Lord's creation of Adam marks humanity's utter reliance on the earth. Once formed, organic matter and water will cycle through his body continually to sustain life. The Lord brings in a last essential element, pushing his own breath into Adam's lungs with his mouth (Genesis 2:7). Respiration symbolizes another site of constant exchange between living souls and the earth's physical matter. This sharing of breath is also a marker of Adam's dependence on the Lord's voice and of other human needs that are to be met by the power of speech. While this breath of life is often explained using a body-soul approach that is dualistic, there is no need for such a distinction. Embodied lips, ears, and vibrating air particles are the workings of speech and breathing. The breath of life enlivens spirit *and* body, creating unified souls.

After Adam's creation, it would seem the two beings stand on a bare mud earth. The Lord has seen to it that there should be no rain or cultivated plant life until a human being is on the earth to till the ground (Genesis 2:5). Adam is to labor and care for creation in a way comparable to the Lord's own efforts. Like God, Adam will penetrate the ground with his hands, sowing and nurturing life. Adam's early creation grants him the privilege of witnessing the unfolding of life on earth. Just after Adam's body is formed, "the Lord God planted a garden" eastward on earth, in Eden (Genesis 2:8). With the slowness and simplicity of hand-sown seeds, mud, and sunlight, the Lord models his work of creating life.

Perhaps the cultivation of the garden, although hardly mentioned in the text at hand, should nevertheless be considered the primal and most intimate revelation of creation. The Lord introduces himself to Adam—as he later will to Moses, Enoch, and others—first and foremost as a creator and sustainer of natural and human life. Even baring soiled hands, the Lord shares some measure of his light and intelligence with Adam. When the Lord revealed himself to Moses, he showed him every soul on earth and even every "particle" of matter on the earth (Moses 1:27–28). The Lord explained that only through seeing all of these things could Moses witness his glory (Moses 1:4–5). The Lord is so enmeshed in his fields of labor that no words or image of self could adequately reveal him.[1] Creation is like an extension of his soul beyond the boundaries of the body, or like a garment that clothes him with glory and light.

Adam's soul, like the Lord's, is to extend into the created world. Adam Miller recently focused on a concept expressed in George Handley's book *Home Waters* as follows: "If the body is like a river, the soul is a watershed."[2] Human souls, or spirits and bodies woven and growing together, are highly "porous" in relation to nature and each other. In flux biologically, culturally, and in countless other ways, human beings receive a constant flow of nourishment and detriment from the physical world. We are grown by interactions with all kinds of entities present and past. In turn, we carve out and sustain others. We are each rivers fed and feeding into the courses of other bodies of water.[3]

---

1. James E. Faulconer, "Self-Image, Self-Love, and Salvation," *Latter-day Digest* (1993), http://jamesfaulconer.byu.edu/papers/self_image.pdf.

2. Adam S. Miller, *Rube Goldberg Machines: Essays in Mormon Theology* (Salt Lake City: Greg Kofford Books, 2012), 50.

3. George B. Handley, *Home Waters: A Year of Recompenses on the Provo River* (Salt Lake City: University of Utah Press, 2010), xi–xvii; Miller, *Rube Goldberg Machines*, 50–53.

In that our souls are like watersheds, human beings are like the Lord. His creations are a vast watershed even more permeable and expansive than ours—a multitude of diverse sites of interchange. Each flows in and out of his thoughts, desires, and sensations. Eden could be considered a "watershed" prepared for Adam. Not only is there food to sustain his body, but also all kinds of creations to "enliven the soul" (D&C 59:19). George Handley borrows the term *home waters* from fly fishing to explain how personal relationships with natural places feed us in a variety of ways. Home waters quench the soul's thirst for sensation, joy, strength, and healing. They sustain capacities to feel emotion, to create meanings, and to engage and produce art. They replenish spiritual sensitivity.

Recompensing creation by sustaining and cultivating life

Having a watershed, however, requires much of us, as it did of Adam. Drinking from the springs and catching the fish of our home waters require living in committed relationships with places and their ecologies. Nature and its life-sustaining systems, Handley explains, can function only through balanced exchanges, or "recompenses." Consequences, returns, and demands perpetually result from what is given and taken. We must sow in order to reap, and we will eat and drink of the same quality of recompenses we offer. Recompensing nature requires opening our eyes and consciously seeking greater knowledge of places, fishing for whatever unseen catches may pull our lines and prove to be important discoveries concerning the needs and unique features of our "home waters."

The Lord sets the quintessential example of giving and receiving life-sustaining recompenses. His competence to create and support life is cultivated by intimate and thorough knowledge. "The Lord *by wisdom* hath founded the earth; *by understanding* hath he established the heavens" (Proverbs 3:19–20, emphasis added). He tells Moses that "all things are numbered unto me, for they are mine, and I know them all" (Moses 1:35). His eyes can pierce and his hands can hold all his workmanship (Moses 7:36). It seems consistent with the spirit of Christ's teachings to neglect and exclude no one and to assert no unrighteous power in governing human and nonhuman life (Matthew 5:39–44). The falling of a sparrow is not excluded from his mindfulness, much less a human being who falters (Matthew 10:29). As a creator of earth as a new world in Genesis 2, the Lord is a pioneer and planter of new knowledge, or an expander of the geographical bounds of his "watershed." Creation is to him like a seedbed of intelligence, glory, and knowledge (D&C 93:36; Moses 1:39).

From the beginning of Adam's time in Eden, his tasks on earth are knowledge oriented and ecological. We read that Adam is "put" in the garden "to dress it and to keep it" in the same short breath (Genesis 2:15). Thus, responsibility to learn about and sustain natural entities comes with entry to the garden, even before the increased responsibilities that will come after partaking of the fruit. Adam is not a mindless physical laborer as he puts his back into tilling and likely many of the other demanding and dirty jobs of gardening. He must also watch and learn in order to maintain the well-being of other living, developing creations; this is the "keeping" part of his stewardship. Only through purposeful observation can he learn to attend to the particular needs of his habitat and the plants and creatures within it. After Adam witnesses the creation of animals, the Lord asks him to choose suitable names, an assignment requiring both reason and imagination (Genesis 2:19). Adam's practice must have been to him as challenging as that of any beginning bird-watcher, botanical artist, or zookeeper. His is the work of gaining ecological literacy, the personal, hands-on care and skill to sustain systems of life. To Adam personally, the Lord has demonstrated such skills in sowing and nurturing the garden and its animals. Adam is a partaker of knowledge concerning many other beings in his home waters.

The knowledge paradox surrounding the tree of knowledge

Yet God warns Adam that the richest source of knowledge in Eden, a fruit-bearing tree, is dangerous. Adam is now faced with a paradox: living with the Lord within the garden requires him to gain and apply knowledge, but the attainment of knowledge will separate him from God. Another facet of this contradictory relationship with knowledge is that although Adam and Eve are intended to find joy in the garden while learning to care for each other and the creations there, love and joy are fed by knowledge. We cannot properly care for or enjoy what we do not know. Only by forsaking life in Eden could Adam begin to pursue its full enjoyment and responsibilities. Perhaps the basic reason behind the paradox is that the process of gaining knowledge necessitates an indefinite state of partial knowledge. Partial knowledge is partial darkness. In this condition individuals become accountable while, at the same time, errors and unwitting violence offensive to God and harmful to life become inevitable.

Although he warns against the dangers of the tree, the Lord is nevertheless its planter and keeper. Perhaps the tree is present, in part, because he eats of it himself. Variations of this tree may spring up wherever he sets foot. Considering his prohibition to Adam, it is as if the fruit ripens in Eden prematurely, before an intended time when the Lord might have guided or commanded Adam to taste it.

Knowledge as fruit

How does plucking and eating fruit resemble learning experiences? First, fruit and knowledge are often both deliberately sought and chosen. We single out particular fruits in a way that's not possible when inhaling air or drinking water from a flowing source. The pursuit of knowledge, at least some kinds, is comparable to seeking a vibrant and enticing object like fruit.

Second, fruit and knowledge often involve comparing tastes and ripeness. We learn to judge quality—to tell which sources of knowledge are metaphorically bruised, pest-ridden, or so overripe they should be cast away. We choose our branches of study as a matter of taste and personal preference, while also rejecting what is unappealing or out-of-date.

Third, knowledge is partaken of multiple times and preserved. Knowledge, like food, nourishes and needs to be continually replenished. One harvest will lead to the plucking, consuming, and storing of other harvests. Knowledge can be processed in a variety of ways for preservation, a skill learned through attentive trial and error. If uncared for and unused, knowledge will rot and mold; seasons bear time-sensitive fruits. Even when we *do* succeed at storing up knowledge, we are never finished with this task; we will labor with our fruit trees as they bear again.

Fourth, fruit contains seeds. We cannot foresee what may grow and where once we spit out or digest them. One taste of knowledge might be the beginning of generations of other trees that sustain us and our communities. We can even attempt to create new cross-pollinated varieties. We plant and breed seeds of trees we particularly love, like preparing resources and spaces for future learning. We know trees by their fruits (Matthew 7:20). To taste and judge a fruit is to judge a tree and to create a relationship with that species. We decide whether to plant and fertilize, ignore, or destroy trees' respective seeds and saplings. We cast away bad branches, striving to cultivate the variety of fruits we prefer and desire. As with fruits, the process of cultivating knowledge is always beyond the horizons of our mastery; we cannot force knowledge to bear truths or evidence according to our will.

Fifth, we cannot know the taste of fruit or its effects on our bodies until we consume. Partaking entails risk. Through experience, we grow leery of the worms in apples and the markings of toxic forest berries. Some fruits are indeed poisonous enough to cause death. The pursuit of knowledge, too, sometimes carries personal moral dangers that we learn to guard against.

Last, like gathering and eating food, the cultivation and partaking of knowledge engages our faculties holistically—eyes, noses, thoughts and desires, hands, stomachs, and other hidden workings of our bodies and spirits all move in this process. It is a fully embodied and mindful event of perceiving, judging, partaking, and transforming. Knowledge is internalized in us and becomes a source of energy and action. For good or bad, its flesh becomes our flesh. Knowledge fuels the actions we take in the physical world. Knowledge nourishes the fruits, or the works that our lives bear up, whether unto life or death (Helaman 14:31).

Partaking of the fruit of ecological wisdom

Every fruit in the garden could be said to impart some form of knowledge; every embodied event and action offers fragments of intelligence about the workings of creation. The physical world satisfies hunger for understanding. Adam keeps the prohibition concerning the tree of knowledge for a time. After Eve is created in the garden, he continues to labor there, and he shares with her the warning given to him from God. This seems apparent when Eve shares a slightly altered version of the prohibition with the serpent: Adam and Eve must not even touch the tree's fruit, lest they suffer death (Genesis 3:3). Eve senses that knowledge is indispensable to embodiment; even just to touch something is enough to gain some understanding of it and form a consequential relationship. Tasting might not even be necessary in order to be influenced by this tree. Adam and Eve initially refrain from partaking of the tree's fruit, but haven't they been gaining knowledge of the physical world all along as they worked in the garden? As they labor and watch, they have been recompensed with the beginnings of understanding. Eve and Adam have entered states of partial knowledge even before they partake of the forbidden fruit.

If, as I suggest, all fruits in Eden impart knowledge, what is special about the fruit of the knowledge of good and evil? Assuming Eve already has access to other flavorful varieties of knowledge, what motivates her to taste this particular fruit? Her motivation seems not so much the temptations of Satan as what she sees by closely observing the properties in the fruit. Drawing near the tree, she judges that the fruit is good for food, beautiful, and capable of imparting wisdom (Genesis 3:6). This last property, wisdom, distinguishes the fruit of the knowledge of good and evil from all else the garden provides.

Wisdom is a qualitatively distinct form of knowledge. If knowledge is the tree of embodied human experience, wisdom is its crowning and sweetest fruit. Wisdom happens when knowledge-imparting experiences grow into a capacity to exercise moral judgment. Wisdom is knowledge applied to the actions that sustain life. It is possible to partake of knowledge without seeking and partaking of wisdom, just as it was possible to hold many other kinds of fruit in Eden without touching the tree of knowledge of good and evil or its fruit.

Eve's desire for wisdom is pertinent to the ecological knowledge Adam and Eve are gaining in the garden. How might we define ecological wisdom? Wisdom in relation to nature involves something beyond understanding how the physical world works and what it needs, even in great detail. Ecological wisdom involves the ripening and outgrowth of knowledge of the natural world into commitment and love. It is faithful stewardship and charity offered to creation and all living things. Even before partaking of the fruit, it appears knowledge has already begun to enlarge Adam and Eve's capacities to feel invested in other souls and entities of creation. Through knowing, they are empowered to love. Adam's experience naming the animals, for example, allows him to gain familiarity with and affection toward God's creations.

Eve also must have learned to love the living things and beauties in Eden. I imagine Eve partaking of the fruit hoping for greater joy, skill, and understanding in her efforts to cultivate life on earth as both a parent and a steward. We should not separate her desire for motherhood from ecological stewardship. To raise a family is to establish an interdependent relationship with the physical world. Parenthood necessitates becoming more responsible for the maintenance and future well-being of natural systems and the water, air, plants, and relationships that allow human bodies to survive with health.

Perhaps Eve consciously aspires to become like God and to walk in the confidence, light, and intelligence he walks in as both Father and Creator. Hunger for wisdom and sheer curiosity outweigh impending dangers in her judgment. She is not certain death will come, how the fruit will taste, or what its effect on her body will be.

Her response to tasting the fruit is significant. Wisdom is not only good for food but also unusually delicious. There is no doubt that she will hunger for it again or that Adam will also enjoy it. She wants wisdom as a staple in their diet. We often imagine the partaking as one small juicy bite for each person, but perhaps they ate several fruits apiece and picked a bushel. The fruit is like an alternative version of the "fruit tree of life." It nourishes capacities to perceive, feel, and know. It is a staff of life. As Eve offers the fruit to Adam, I imagine him gauging his levels of commitment to her and feeling conflicted. Refraining from the fruit was easy when he was alone and less experienced, but now that he has formed interdependent relationships with Eve and other living beings in the garden, he is shaken. He trusts Eve's judgment and taste and allows her to prick his appetite. Adam and Eve have developed some degree of loyalty; he is more willing to partake knowing that Eve has tasted and may be separated from him.

Choosing the fruit demonstrates a comparable oneness with and loyalty to creation. It is as if by eating the fruit of knowledge, Eve and Adam accept and embrace earth and their embodied life for all it is and all it offers—every recompense both gifted and required, every ray of knowledge, emotion, and sensation.

Sweet, bitter, and soul-enlarging effects of the fruit

However, besides the profound sweetness of eating, other initial effects of the fruit are bitter. Ignorance distinguished Adam and Eve from God even before partaking. But now they become more keenly aware that they have long been ignorant and are still partially ignorant. What they see first is what is most immediate and personal—their own nakedness. They grow fearful of the gaps that differentiate them from the glory and wisdom that clothes the Lord. Both parties draw veils: Adam and Eve in hiding and attempting to clothe themselves with fig leaves, and the Lord in barring them from the tree of life and Eden (Genesis 3:7–8, 23–24). Perhaps the tree of knowledge of good and evil was a fig tree. This would enhance the potency of these leaves as a symbol of knowledge and make the choice of Adam and Eve to independently partake of the tree obvious as they stand before the Lord.

Distance from the Lord is unpleasant, but it also makes visible new possible paths toward progression. The knowledge gap was always there, but now Adam and Eve are empowered to deliberately address it. Unexpectedly, it is sometimes our very awareness of a veil between us and the Lord that makes it possible for us to receive the Lord's grace and draw closer to his presence. Veils invite us to see and confess our weakness before God, and this prepares us to receive his counsel and strength.[4]

---

4. Miller, *Rube Goldberg Machines*, 101–5.

Adam and Eve receive strength in this moment of weakness by speaking with the Lord. God's words enlarge their willingness to become faithful and wise stewards into full accountability and commitment before him. God imparts a bitter and sweet helping of wisdom concerning what is to come on earth. Adam and Eve are promised the joys and sorrows of marriage, parenthood, hard work, growing food, creating homes, facing chaos in the natural world, and death. Having digested the seeds of wisdom, they are now free to plant and nurture new sources of this substance with the Lord's assistance from afar. In order to plant their own gardens, they return to the muddy grounds where God created Adam. This is a much greater trust than Eden; the potential bounds of home and sources of knowledge expand from one section of the river flowing through a garden to the river's sources, its four branches, and all distributaries. Even more of the knowledge of God can be obtained here than in Eden if they will actively seek it. God's fruit of wisdom proves to be the substance of mortal life. Opposition imparts wisdom and resilience against the deceptions of Satan (Genesis 3:15–19). Through faithful stewardship and endurance, they may be recompensed with knowledge in every harsh and mild season on earth. The Lord dresses them with knowledge and wisdom much as he clothes them with apparel that compensates for the limitations of their fig leaf aprons (Genesis 3:21).

Parting veils of ignorance as stewards

Veils of human ignorance about how to care for creation can be parted through the humble pursuit of ecological wisdom. Approaching such barriers is pertinent to building communities in the Lord's way. As we do so, we can be filled with a greater measure of the Lord's knowledge and compassion.

In the midst of establishing Zion, the prophet Enoch experienced two soul-enlarging visions that revealed human evil and its impact on creation. The Lord weeps while witnessing the violence with Enoch. He explains that he gives his children knowledge and agency so that they might love and care for others; nevertheless, many of his children choose hatred (Moses 7:32–33). Enoch witnesses how "all the workmanship of [God's] hands" grieve with God. Even the soul of the earth itself suffers. All is sentient. Enoch is saturated with charity for all forms of life, human and nonhuman. Enoch "wept and stretched forth his arms, and his heart swelled wide as eternity; and his bowels yearned; and all eternity shook" (Moses 7:41). He recognizes the extent of his entanglement in the events in the vision. These are his relatives, he indicates (Moses 6:43). This burdened earth is his home, even the lifeblood of Zion.

Enoch's bitter knowledge is a soul-gorging fountain of information, sensation, and feeling. He despairs, but then the Lord commands him to rejoice as he shows him the ministry of Jesus Christ. In the process of witnessing Christ's atonement, Enoch responds with joy, crying, "The Righteous is lifted up, and the Lamb is slain from the foundation of the world; and through faith, I am in the bosom of the Father, and behold, Zion is with me" (Moses 7:47). Facing the minutiae and totality of evil on earth fills him with more complete knowledge of the expansiveness of Christ's suffering and redemptive powers. Enoch comes to know that Zion must aspire to live and labor in ways that rise above all forms of violence. He sees that it is only through Christ's great recompense that humanity can become wise. Enoch's heart expands in charity toward the infinity and eternity of God's creations.

We can be strengthened by Enoch's example of resisting any temptation to block the flow of knowledge of the physical world. Ignorance would have stunted his mission to clothe and beautify Zion. Today, our souls are fed by watersheds that are global, opaque, and confusing. It is tempting to let capacities to observe relationships in the physical world atrophy. Yet such neglect can impede the expansion, charity, and joy of our souls. If we cultivate self-image rather than knowledge and charity, we starve ourselves of sustenance and invite harmful recompenses of any unwitting violence.[5] Self-imposed veils[6] of ecological ignorance cannot block the ebb and flow of the surging world that shapes us. We, like Enoch, are free to deliberately choose to seek to part such veils and let our hearts expand with charity through knowledge.

---

5. Handley, *Home Waters*, xii.
6. Miller, *Rube Goldberg Machines*, 105.

Stewardship: Bitter cup or sweet fruit?

Too often environmental stewardship has been pushed aside like an undesirable or bitter cup in Latter-day Saint families. In Utah Valley, for example, a lack of informed and committed stewardship has led communities to neglect and harm life-sustaining resources. Receding, contaminated, and overused freshwater supplies call into question the sustainability of communities in the valley.[7] Air pollution continues to worsen, adversely affecting quality of life and health for all.[8] In relation to such crises, we fail to appreciate two things about bitter cups: first, they are usually unavoidable; and second, as for Enoch, such cups are soul-enlarging experiences. We forget that "to the hungry soul every bitter thing is sweet" (Proverbs 27:7).

Instead of being a bitter cup, could environmental education and stewardship become something more like partaking of the fruit of the tree of knowledge? Through closer study, could we as communities in Zion discern that it is "good for food," "pleasant to our eyes," and "desirable to make us wise"? (compare Genesis 3:6). If we pay greater attention to the fruits of ecological wisdom and how they might draw us and future generations closer to the Lord, might we discover that our souls are famished for this substance? Committed stewardship is a more abundant source of sustenance for human souls than we have imagined. This neglected field in Zion holds the promise of veil-parting experiences, greater knowledge of God, and greater charity for us and our children.

Greater knowledge and commitment as stewards might help us have a greater appreciation of the Lord's role as a creator and sustainer of life, even though such knowledge can bring pain and difficulties. As we see in Enoch's vision, sustaining the Lord's creations doesn't bring only peace and joy to the Lord. Enoch witnesses how the Lord doesn't shield himself from a full knowledge of his creation or the emotions that come with these relationships. The Lord's way of life is not centered on efficiency, convenience, or comfort. Perhaps he frequently partakes

---

7. Handley, *Home Waters*, 14–16.
8. Handley, *Home Waters*, 89.

of bitter gushes of the knowledge of violence that he shared with Enoch, while yet being recompensed by fruits that affirm his consistent preference for life and light. So it can be for us as builders of Zion today. Our souls can be enlivened even in the midst of clouds of darkness and the indifference of natural forces. Even negative consequences we reap from others' past mistakes can lead to increased compassion and understanding.[9]

Environmental education in Zion

Teaching private practices of recycling and decreased consumption is not enough to provide children with spiritual hope and competence as future stewards. Children need our help in preparing to address environmental challenges with knowledge and skill on personal and community levels.[10] Leaders and parents in Zion will need to enrich and augment environmental education for youth. Like Adam and Eve, children need guides who are wiser and more prepared than they are. With our help, they can partake of soul-enlarging learning experiences at school, as they serve the greater public society, and as they labor in Zion.

Latter-day Saint communities already cultivate many of the essential ingredients of environmental education among youth, including the application of problem-solving skills in local communities and empathetic imagination. There are two specific practices we have not yet adopted, however, that are essential if we are to become wise and informed mentors of children as environmental stewards: (1) the active, curious, and joyful pursuit of ecological understanding; and (2) the application of charity and empathy to environmental problems, toward both human and nonhuman life. Personal empathy for natural life and personal understanding of how ecosystems sustain life form the backbone of moral competence in caring for the natural world.[11] Paired with

---

9. Handley, *Home Waters*, 89.

10. See Louise Chawla and Debra Flanders Cushing, "Education for Strategic Environmental Behavior," *Environmental Education Research* 13/4 (2007): 437–52.

11. Daniel Goleman, Lisa Bennett, and Zenobia Barlow, *Ecoliterate: How Educators Are Cultivating Emotional, Social, and Ecological Intelligence* (San Francisco: Jossey-Bass, 2012), 7.

service, sacrifice, and leadership skills, greater spiritual and intellectual mindfulness of the workings of life and ecology is needed. Deliberately cultivating these values can empower us and future generations to become more assertive, informed, and spiritually minded stewards of creation in every level of society we labor in.

As we seek to become more attentive to the natural world, we will each see that we are not yet fully clothed with as much knowledge or charity as we need. While such realizations are never comfortable, we should celebrate our efforts to learn. Adults can find great joy in experiencing childlike curiosity and wonder about natural systems *with* children.[12]

Humble openness to new perspectives is key to becoming true stewards and mentors. Throughout *Home Waters*, George Handley describes how learning to care for natural habitats requires deliberate "receptivity." We should willingly seek to expose our lives to whatever may prove relevant to sustaining the unique gifts of our natural watersheds. This pursuit is akin to fishing. We cannot foresee what particular encounters, stories, or observations may suddenly pull our lines and prove provident. Family histories, for example, may strengthen our capacities and commitments as stewards. Yet stories outside our personal heritages also play crucial roles in shattering complacency and false assumptions. In order to effectively care for the land, scientific understanding and practical skill should also be sought and utilized. We should know the names and needs of species sustained by local natural systems and how human actions affect these habitats.[13] Simple changes in our minds and hearts can make what was imperceptible visible and tangible. Gaining knowledge, we increase in our competence to "prepare every needful thing" (D&C 109:8) to fulfill our purpose to enjoy life on earth with gratitude and integrity.

As we taste the fruits of ecological wisdom, we will perceive the unique ways these fruits have developed and sweetened in our dispensation. Although being enmeshed in global communities burdens us

---

12. Richard Louv, *Last Child in the Woods: Saving Our Children from Nature-Deficit Disorder* (Chapel Hill, NC: Algonquin Books of Chapel Hill, 2008).

13. Handley, *Home Waters*.

heavily as stewards, it also expands the watersheds that sustain our souls. To relate to more of the Lord's beloved creations with open eyes, ears, and hands is to witness and receive more of his glory (Moses 1:5). Our yoke can be made easy (Matthew 11:30); sweet and joyful recompenses will come if we take up this fruit with charity and the desire to become more like the Lord. Cultivating "faithful and wise" stewardship among ourselves and our youth may empower them to become vital beacons of hope and exemplars of good stewardship in generations to come (Luke 12:42–43).

Contributors

James E. Faulconer is a Fellow at the Wheatley Institution, Brigham Young University, where he has taught since 1975. A former Richard L. Evans Professor of Religious Understanding, Faulconer has a PhD in philosophy focusing on contemporary European philosophy. He and Janice Allen are the parents of four and the grandparents of fourteen. Besides writing books and articles in philosophy, Jim is the author of the "Made Harder" series of books for scripture study and *The Life of Holiness*.

Adam S. Miller is a professor of philosophy at Collin College in McKinney, Texas. He earned a PhD in philosophy from Villanova University. He is the author of six books, including *Letters to a Young Mormon* (Maxwell Institute, 2013), *The Gospel According to David Foster Wallace* (Bloomsbury, 2016), and *Future Mormon* (Kofford, 2016). He directs the Mormon Theology Seminar and coedits a series of books for the Maxwell Institute entitled Groundwork: Studies in Theory and Scripture.

Julie M. Smith graduated from the University of Texas at Austin with a BA in English and from the Graduate Theological Union in Berkeley, California, with an MA in biblical studies. She is on the executive board of the Mormon Theology Seminar and on the steering committee for the BYU New Testament Commentary, for which she is writing a commentary on the Gospel of Mark. She is the author of *Search, Ponder, and Pray: A Guide to the Gospels.* Julie is married to Derrick Smith; they live near Austin, Texas, where she homeschools their three children. She also blogs for Times & Seasons, where she is the book review editor.

BEN SPACKMAN is pursuing a PhD at Claremont Graduate University in the history of Christianity and religion. He has a BA in Near Eastern studies (BYU) and has done MA and PhD work in Semitics (University of Chicago) as well as formal scientific study (City College of New York). His research focuses on the book of Genesis in the ancient and modern world, the history of science, evolution, and scriptural interpretation.

JOSEPH M. SPENCER is a visiting assistant professor of ancient scripture at Brigham Young University. He is the author of three books: *An Other Testament, For Zion,* and, most recently, *The Vision of All: Twenty-Five Lectures on Isaiah in Nephi's Record.* He serves also as the associate director of the Mormon Theology Seminar and is currently the editor of the *Journal of Book of Mormon Studies.* He and Karen, his wife, live in Provo, Utah, with their five children.

ROSALYNDE WELCH is an independent scholar working in Mormon literature, culture, and theology. She holds a PhD in early modern English literature from the University of California at San Diego. Her work has appeared in *BYU Studies, Dialogue, Element, Journal of Book of Mormon Studies,* and other journals and edited volumes. She lives in St. Louis, Missouri, with her husband and four children.

CANDICE D. WENDT lives in Montreal, Québec, with her husband, Dennis, a professor at McGill University. She received her MA in comparative studies from Brigham Young University in 2009. Candice has been an at-home parent for eight years and plans to pursue a teaching career. She is currently studying French with her children.